Here's what people are saying about The Mystery Shopper's Manual:

"We tell our newly-hired office staff and shoppers to read Cathy Stucker's *The Mystery Shopper's Manual* to take the MYSTERY out of mystery shopping."
— **Christopher Warzynski**
Vice President, Beyond Hello Inc.

"If you read only one book about the secrets of mystery shopping, this book must be your choice."
— **Chuck Paul**
President, A Closer Look

"*The Mystery Shopper's Manual* is a valuable resource, with real world tips and advice from a professional who has been there, done that. I highly recommend it."
— **John Saccheri**
Founder and CEO, Mystique Shopper

"Cathy Stucker's book reveals both the high standards shopping companies require as well as the no-nonsense tactics that make shoppers profitable quickly. Her book is a must read for those who want to be savvy in the mystery shopping community. "
— **Paige Hall**
President, The Secret Shopper Company

11.03

"If you want to know what mystery shopping companies are looking for, *The Mystery Shopper's Manual* is a must read!"

—Lana L. Lenzini
Vice President, Professional Review &
Operational Shoppers, Inc.

"Mystery shopping, when properly executed and documented, will have a significant effect in a business environment; from the attitude and livelihood of the staff to their impact on future guest sales and service experiences. If you're willing to make the commitment to GET INVOLVED in our industry, then READ THIS MANUAL."

—Michael Bare – ISHC
President - Bare Associates International Inc.
Co-Founder / Past President of the MSPA

"A must-read for anyone who is serious about becoming a professional shopper and strives to be a mystery shopping company's "first choice" for assignments."

—Susan Seiler
President, SG Marketing Group, Inc.

"*The Mystery Shopper's Manual* will help you to perform excellent shops in a professional manner."

—Beverly Gleason
Owner, Mystery Shoppers

"Forget the hype about making big money, eating for free and taking cruises. Here you get the truth and well-researched advice on what can be a great career or profitable spare-time hobby."

—Raymond F. Sola
Founder and President Volition.com LLC

The Mystery Shopper's Manual cuts through the hype and gets to the nitty-gritty of mystery shopping. Cathy's book provided the information I needed to get started. If you're serious about mystery shopping, this is the book for you!"

—Jo Adamson
MSPA Gold Certified Mystery Shopper

The Mystery Shopper's Manual is a highly lucrative and "user friendly" guide to getting a rewarding part-time, full-time or spare-time mystery shopping job!"

—Midwest Book Review

"This book is educational and factual and can help the beginning or intermediate mystery shopper with obtaining more shops, writing better reports, and other useful information. I would highly recommend it to anyone even remotely interested in doing shopping for money!"

—Amazon.com reader review

"If you're intrigued by the idea of getting paid to shop, this is the book for you. I found several shops—and they more than covered the cost of the book—in the first week I owned it. Nice and concise!"

"The Mystery Shopper's Manual (5th edition)" chosen "2003 Mystery Shopping Industry Book of the Year"

The

sixth edition

Mystery Shopper's

MANUAL

The

sixth edition

Mystery Shopper's

MANUAL

How to get paid
to shop in your
favorite stores,
eat in your
favorite
restaurants,
and more!

Cathy Stucker

**Special Interests Publishing
Sugar Land, Texas**

The Mystery Shopper's Manual:
How to get paid to shop in your favorite stores, eat in your favorite restaurants, and more!

Published by:
Special Interests Publishing
4646 Hwy 6, #123
Sugar Land, TX 77478

Orders: 1-888-BOOK-888 (888-266-5888)

Royalty-free articles on mystery shopping, publishing, small business marketing and other topics are available at http://www.idealady.com/content.htm.

For more information on mystery shopping, visit Cathy Stucker on the Internet at http://www.IdeaLady.com/.

Cover design © 2004 TLC Graphics
www.TLCGraphics.com

Printed in the United States of America
Library of Congress Control Number: 2004095179
ISBN 1-888983-30-2

*This book is dedicated to
my husband, Michael,
for always understanding and
encouraging me to reach for my dreams.*

Acknowledgments

Many people generously shared their knowledge during the research and writing of this book. Information and time were contributed by Eric Brooks of Archon Development, Michael Bare of Bare Associates International/Video Eyes, Tina San Roman of Coast to Coast Scheduling, Joanna Ellis of Ellis Property Management, Howard Levinson of Howard Services/Service Sleuths, Lorri Kern of Kern Scheduling Services, Kimberly Nasief of Marketing Endeavors, John Saccheri of Mystique Shopper, Lana Lenzini and Lori Gully of Professional Review & Operational Shoppers, Inc., Charles Kenerson of QSI Specialists, Jeff Hall and Karmen Saran of Second to None, Bob and Susan Seiler of SG Marketing, Mike Green of Speedmark Information Services, John Hsu of Surf Merchants, Tracey Conners of The Corporate Research Group, Paige Hall of The Secret Shopper Company, Sherry Fox of YourWebness.com, and others. Special thanks go to each of them for helping to make this book informative, realistic and useful to mystery shoppers.

Many mystery shoppers, as well as those who have been mystery shopped, shared their experiences with me. Thank you to all of you.

Thanks to Tamara Dever and Erin Stark of TLC Graphics for the great cover design. And thanks to all of my friends and colleagues who provided input and feedback on the book.

Disclaimer:
Please Read

This book is designed to provide helpful and informative material about the mystery shopping business. The publisher and author are not engaged in rendering professional legal, accounting or other services in this book. If the reader requires personal assistance or advice, a qualified professional should be consulted.

It is the responsibility of the mystery shopper to abide by any licensing requirements or other laws which may exist regarding mystery shopping.

Mystery shopping is not a get-rich-quick scheme. The amount of income earned by a mystery shopper depends on many factors, including the shopper's geographic location, prior experience, availability to work, and ability and willingness to perform to required standards. Most mystery shoppers should not expect to rely on mystery shopping to generate all of their income. The author and publisher make no guarantees regarding the number of mystery shopping assignments a shopper may receive or the income to be derived.

Every effort has been made to make the information herein as accurate and complete as possible. However, there may be typographical or other mistakes. Information which was correct at the time of publication may become inaccurate with the passage of time as the industry evolves.

The author and publisher shall have no liability or responsibility to any person or entity with respect to any loss or damage caused, or alleged to be caused, directly or indirectly, by use or misuse of the information in this book.

Table of Contents

Foreword

Would you like to be able to ask mystery shopping companies and schedulers how you can get more assignments? How to get your first shop with a company? How you can make your reports better? There aren't enough hours in the day for companies to take questions from the hundreds of thousands of people interested in mystery shopping; however, Cathy Stucker has asked them the things you want to know. She has also asked the questions you might not know to ask, but need the answers to nonetheless.

Mystery shopping is a competitive business, and it is becoming more competitive all the time. The shoppers who will succeed are those who understand that mystery shopping is a business, act professionally, and constantly seek to improve their skills.

Cathy Stucker's book, *The Mystery Shopper's Manual*, describes how you can become—and remain—a successful shopper. Reading this book will give you the inside story from people who are leaders in the mystery shopping industry, people who know Cathy and share her mission of improving the quality and reputation of mystery shoppers and mystery shopping. You will learn what you can do to build relationships with mystery shopping companies and schedulers, and how to avoid damaging those relationships.

Recently, there has been an overload of information about mystery shopping available on the Internet, in books and ebooks, through continuing education courses and other sources. While some of what you will learn elsewhere is good information, many of these sources contain inaccuracies and misconceptions—inaccuracies that can cost you shops and waste your time.

Cathy Stucker was selected by the Mystery Shopping Providers Association (the world's leading mystery shopping trade association) to help develop and present our Mystery Shopper Gold Certification Workshops because she tells the truth about mystery shopping without the hype and unrealistic expectations. You won't get rich as a mystery shopper, but it is possible to make extra money to help with your family's bills, supplement your retirement income, or possibly even make a living as a professional shopper.

Although being a mystery shopper can be exciting and fun, the day-to-day work of mystery shopping can sometimes be demanding. Lining up and planning assignments, dealing with the unexpected, and writing reports each present their own challenges.

That's when the valuable information and dose of inspiration you will find in these pages will come in handy.

The Mystery Shopper's Manual is a valuable addition to any shopper's library. It is a reference you will find yourself turning to again and again for advice, tips, and inspiration. I wish that all shoppers (both new and experienced) would take the time to read this book before conducting their next shops.

Lorri Kern
MSPA Shopper Services Committee Chair
Founder and President, Kern Scheduling Services
http://www.kernscheduling.com/

What is Mystery Shopping?

Mystery shoppers visit businesses "disguised as normal customers," and do the things other customers do—ask questions, make a purchase, make a return—but with a twist. These undercover customers are there to evaluate the businesses and their employees. After a visit, the mystery shopper completes a report or questionnaire detailing what occurred during the visit.

Mystery shopping goes by many names, including secret shopping, service evaluation, service check and others. No matter what it's called, mystery shopping is an important tool for businesses that care about how they are perceived by customers.

Why Do Businesses Hire Mystery Shoppers?

Shops have different objectives. In general, shops are done to find out about the level of service provided to customers. However, mystery shoppers may also be asked to verify that employees are neatly groomed and in uniform, the business is clean and merchandise is displayed neatly, staff persons are knowledgeable, etc. As a mystery shopper, you may be asked to verify if employees used a certain phrase (such as, "Thank you for shopping at Mega Mart.") or if they used suggestive selling techniques ("Would you like fries with that?").

You may even be asked to shop a client's competitor, so the client can compare their operations to others'. Mystery shoppers may monitor pricing, or verify that the business is in compliance with professional standards or government regulations.

One common misconception about mystery shoppers is that they are just looking for what is wrong. In fact, a mystery shopper is there to provide an objective view of the business, and they report on the good as well as the not-so-good.

Mystery shoppers seek the answers to questions. Were you greeted when you entered the store? Were the shelves properly stocked? Was the store clean? Did the rest rooms have soap and tissue? Was the salad bar completely stocked with fresh vegetables? How long did it take to be served? Did the salesperson tell you about the available service contract? Did the cashier properly count out your change? After they leave the business, they fill out a form or write a report describing what they observed.

Mystery shopping is not opinion research. Shoppers are not paid to give their opinions, they are paid to report their observations.

When evaluating businesses, mystery shoppers are the eyes and ears of the business owner. Shoppers tell them how customers see the business. Most businesses have service standards and rules for safety and security. As a mystery shopper, you tell the business owner whether his employees are living up to the standards and following the rules.

How Is the Information Used?

Businesses use the information from shopper reports to reward good employees, identify training deficiencies, make stores safer for employees and customers, and much more. Companies may base performance evaluations and bonus pay outs at least in part on the results of mystery shops.

The information obtained in mystery shopping reports allows the business to monitor the performance of one location when compared to another, or how the performance of the same location has improved over time.

Mystery shopping is also valuable for the *sentinel effect*. When employees know that they will be mystery shopped—but they don't know when or by whom—they will give every customer excellent service.

This is especially true when the results of mystery shops are used in employee performance evaluations.

The Need for Mystery Shoppers

Today's business environment is extremely competitive. Companies that fail to provide excellent service will not survive. Studies show that a satisfied customer will tell three other people about his experience. A dissatisfied customer will tell ten to twelve people. All too often, though, the customer won't tell the business owner or manager.

Not only do companies face loss of business from poor service, the actions of their employees may cause them to be sued by customers or fined by the government. With so much at stake, mystery shoppers provide a valuable service by identifying potential problems the business owner can correct before they result in a major liability.

Who Are the Mystery Shoppers?

Because mystery shoppers look like typical customers (and are, in most ways, typical customers) almost anyone can become a mystery shopper. Shoppers may be any (adult) age, male or female. They may be employed, self-employed, unemployed, students, retired or full time homemakers.

What makes mystery shoppers different from other customers is that they want to help improve customer service and make some extra money while doing so, and they are specially prepared to evaluate businesses and report their findings.

Many shoppers get into this business because it is fun. They love to get the perks, such as "free" food and merchandise, and even make a little money while they're getting this free stuff! Although mystery shopping can be fun, it is a business and you will have important responsibilities as a mystery shopper.

If you are interested in working flexible, part time hours, and getting paid to shop, eat and more while providing an important service to businesses, this book can help you. Read on to get the inside story on mystery shopping.

What Do Mystery Shoppers Do?

Now that you know what mystery shopping is and why businesses are mystery shopped, let's go along on a shop to find out what mystery shoppers actually do.

Janice Rogers is watching, taking stock of everything around her, as she pulls into the parking lot. Loose carts, trash, potholes—nothing escapes her attention. As she enters the store, she notices that a greeter is there, saying hello and offering her a cart. She walks through the store to the electronics department. She asks a salesperson, Steve, where she can find video cameras. He points in the direction of a display case and says, "Over there," but does not escort her to the case or offer to show any cameras. Janice asks if he can show her which models are digital. Steve responds to her question and takes several minutes to point out features on the cameras she asked about.

After her encounter with Steve, Janice stops in the rest room. It's clean, but there is no soap in the dispensers. Then, Janice selects a product to purchase and heads for the checkouts. Anna, the cashier, greets Janice with "Good afternoon," and a smile. She rings up Janice's purchase quickly and correctly. Janice pays with a credit card, and as she hands Janice her purchase, Anna says, "Thank you for shopping with us, Mrs. Rogers."

Back in her car, Janice records the whole experience on a report form. From the poor appearance of the parking lot to the excellent service of the cashier, all will be noted.

What just happened here? Janice is a mystery shopper. Her job is to see how well the employees at stores, restaurants, gas stations, banks, and other businesses do their jobs. She will write a report about her shopping trip, including the good and the bad, that will go to store management. In return, she will be paid a fee, plus an allowance for the purchase she made at the store.

This is just one example of how mystery shoppers work. If you have never heard of mystery shopping before, you may be surprised to learn that there are thousands of people who get paid to shop at their favorite stores, then record their observations on a simple report form. Even if you are familiar with the concept of mystery shopping, you may be amazed at the types of businesses which use mystery shoppers, and the opportunities that exist for you.

Who Uses
Mystery Shoppers?

You may think of restaurants or department stores when you think of mystery shopping, but almost any business that deals with the public has a need for mystery shoppers. You will have the opportunity to mystery shop a wide variety of businesses.

Examples of businesses currently using mystery shoppers include:

amusement parks	car rental agencies
apartment complexes	carpet cleaners
automobile dealers	casinos
auto repair shops	cell phone stores
banks	coffee shops
bars and clubs	convenience stores
bookstores	copy and print shops
boutiques	credit unions
bowling alleys	day care centers
brokerage houses	department stores

discount stores
doughnut shops
dry cleaners
fast food chains
financial services
florists
funeral homes
gas stations
gift shops
grocery stores
hair salons
health care providers
health clubs
home builders
home improvement stores
hospitals
hotels and resorts
Internet retailers

marinas
movie theaters
museums
nursing homes
online merchants
outlet malls
restaurants
RV parks
savings & loan companies
self-storage facilities
shoe stores
specialty retail stores
tourist attractions
travel companies
truck and trailer rental
truck stops
video rental stores
vision care providers

Mystery shoppers are also used by the government to check up on the businesses it regulates, and government agencies at all levels use mystery shopping to evaluate the service they provide to their citizen customers.

In addition, vendors and distributors may mystery shop retailers who sell their products in order to determine if the products are properly displayed and that employees are using effective selling techniques.

Do You Have What it Takes to Be a Mystery Shopper?

When mystery shopping companies were asked what makes someone a good mystery shopper, they came up with remarkably similar answers. Several said that their best mystery shoppers are those who care about customer service and want to help businesses improve. Although they like making the extra money and getting the free perks that come with mystery shopping, they truly enjoy the work and aren't in it just for the money.

According to the companies surveyed, a mystery shopper must be:

Reliable.

This is a business, and companies depend on you to complete your shop as assigned. The biggest complaint of mystery shopping companies is that shoppers take assignments, don't do them and don't communicate with the company. In fact, approximately 25% of assignments accepted aren't completed by the shoppers and must be reassigned. Do your shops on time, as you agreed, and you will be off to a good start.

Organized.
You may have to juggle multiple assignments with different requirements and deadlines from more than one company.

Able to Read and Follow Written Guidelines.
Clients have specific requirements about when and how shops are to be completed. You must follow those guidelines in order to complete a valid shop.

Observant.
During a shop you will have to obtain employee names, descriptions, and other details.

Able to Remember Details.
The more information you can retain, the easier it will be to complete quality reports.

Objective.
Mystery shopping is not opinion research, and you are not writing a review. Most questions on a mystery shopping report form are yes/no. Either something happened or it didn't. Something was true or it was not. Simply state the facts.

Flexible.
A shop may have to be done within a short time frame, or the client may require that it be done at a certain time or on a certain day. The more flexible you are about when and where you can shop, the more valuable you are to the mystery shopping company.

Honest.
Clients depend on the information in mystery shopping reports to make important business decisions. Don't try to fake a report or answers on the report. First of all, you should have the integrity to do the shop right. If that's not enough motivation for you, you should know that you will probably be caught. There are ways to verify the information in your report.

Thorough.
Carefully prepare for the shop and know exactly what is expected of you. When doing the shop, do everything you were asked to do and get all of the required information. Completely answer all questions on the form, including appropriate comments and narratives. Check your report for accuracy and completeness before submitting it.

A Good Writer.
The comments and narratives you write should make the reader feel as if they are sharing your experience,

seeing what you saw, and hearing what you heard. You don't need to be a brilliant writer, but you must be able to paint a vivid picture in words. Proper grammar, spelling and punctuation are important.

What Education and Experience Does a Mystery Shopper Need?

Some companies prefer that you already have experience in mystery shopping or consumer research. Most companies don't care whether or not you have experience. One company said that an advantage of using inexperienced shoppers is that they don't have any bad habits that have to be trained out of them!

Some companies give preference to shoppers with experience in the industries they shop. So, if you have worked in retail, hospitality, or other service fields, that gives you an edge.

Most companies don't have specific educational requirements. Some mentioned that better-educated shoppers may have stronger writing skills, but the writing skills are more important than how you got them.

Certification

Although it is not required, many companies give preference to shoppers who have completed the Silver or Gold Certifications offered by the Mystery Shopping Providers Association. The certification programs give a solid grounding in mystery shopping, and completing them shows companies that you have made a commitment to being a professional shopper.

For information about the certification programs, visit the Mystery Shopping Providers Association web site at http://www.mysteryshop.org/certification.php.

What Equipment Does a Shopper Need?

More and more, mystery shopping companies are relying on the Internet to recruit shoppers, make assignments, and receive reports. While it is still possible to get some mystery shopping assignments without a computer or Internet access, it is getting harder all the time.

If you don't have a computer at home, you may be able to use one at work (make sure it's not against company policy) or at your local library. But consider getting a computer and Internet account at home. The cost has come down significantly over the last few years, and because you will use it for business, some or all of the cost may be tax deductible.

Although most reports are now completed using web-based forms, some companies' reports are Microsoft Word or Excel documents. If you have those programs, and know how to use them, it is a plus.

Depending on where you live and the nature of the assignments, some companies will want you to have a driver's license and a car.

Once you get beyond these basic requirements, there aren't a lot of hard and fast rules. Every company has different procedures and requirements, but here are some of the items mentioned as "good to have." That means that they generally aren't required, but it may be a plus if you have them:

Answering machine, voice mail, mobile phone or pager.
If a company needs to reach you (with a question about a report or to make a last-minute assignment) they need to reach you quickly. They don't want to call a number where there is no answer or get a busy signal because you are online.

Scanner.
A scanner is useful for submitting receipts and other paperwork via e-mail. This is the preferred method of submitting receipts to most companies.

Fax.
If you don't have a scanner, you can submit receipts and other paperwork via fax.

Stopwatch (or digital watch with stopwatch).
You may need to time transactions. Timings must be made without drawing attention to yourself, so your stopwatch must be easy to use discreetly.

Digital recorder.
Many shoppers like to use digital recorders on shops. They are able to get verbatim comments of the employees, and the recorders are also useful for getting exact timings. There are also audio shops where a digital recorder is used to record the entire shop.

Digital logger.
This device plugs into your telephone and computer and records directly from your phone line. The recording can then be uploaded as a part of your report or e-mailed to the mystery shopping company.

Digital camera.
Some shops now require that you have a digital camera to take photos of the location, displays, products, etc. Although a digital camera is not required to be a mystery shopper, having one will make you eligible for many shops.

Digital scale, thermometers and other measuring equipment.
Some food and beverage shops will require that you weigh the food items and verify the temperatures at which they were served. Many companies doing these types of shops will want you to use their equipment, but some will allow you to use your own.

The mystery shopping company's application will ask whether you have any of the items that are important to them.

When a company requires the use of specialized equipment, they will often provide it to you. For example, video mystery shops require the use of a miniature camera and recording equipment that can be easily concealed. If you are selected to perform a video shop, they will provide the equipment you need.

Can You Make Money Doing This?

Yes, you can really get paid to shop. Mystery shopping isn't a get-rich-quick scheme, and it's not money for nothing. But mystery shopping can be easy and fun, and it is a great way to make extra money in your spare time while doing things you have to do anyway. You've got to shop and eat, right?

Most assignments can be completed within a range of days and times, so you have flexibility about when you work. You will usually be offered assignments close to your home, or in areas you have indicated you are willing to travel to, so you can do the shops while you are running other errands. Some shoppers are willing to take assignments far from home when they are able to set up routes, with shops all along the way. Many of the shops I do are in stores and restaurants I go to regularly, so I'd be there anyway. This way, I'm getting paid to be there.

How much money you make will depend on how many shops you do and how much you are paid for each shop. When you work as a contract mystery shopper, you can't count on a certain income from month to month.

While some companies may keep you busy, in many cases you will receive only one or two shops from a single company in a month. By contracting with many companies, the number of shops you do and the income you receive could increase.

Pay for mystery shops varies, depending on how much time is required, if any special expertise is needed, and if you receive a reimbursement for goods or services. You may receive a bonus if you accept a hard-to-fill assignment, or a rush job.

Pay Structure

Pay for a mystery shop may be:

Reimbursement only, where you are paid for a required purchase. For example, you may do a restaurant shop where your meal costs for two people are reimbursed with no additional fee paid.

Fee only, where you receive a set fee for completing the shop but there is no purchase reimbursement. This is common for shops where there is no purchase requirement, such as banks and apartment complexes.

Fee plus reimbursement, where you receive both a fee and reimbursement for a required purchase. You may find this when doing retail or restaurant shops, as well as others involving a required purchase.

When you are reimbursed for a required purchase, the purchase allowance may be used for anything you wish, or you may be told to purchase a specific item. In some cases, you may be able to return the item purchased and keep the cash.

Although it's not typical, you may be paid a mileage allowance for some shops. Usually, companies will schedule you for shops near your home or other places you've indicated that you are willing to go. However, there are times when it is hard to locate a shopper in the area. If you are asked to do one of these shops and make a special trip out of your usual area, you may be offered a bonus or mileage allowance.

Most companies do not pay expenses such as postage or fax fees to submit a receipt. They consider this minimal expense part of your fee, and don't make a separate reimbursement. Many companies have toll-free fax lines or allow you to scan and e-mail receipts to them, so you would not have to incur any expense.

Fees and Reimbursements

There is no such thing as a "typical" mystery shopping fee. The requirements for each shop are different, and so are each company's policies. *The fee ranges mentioned here are for illustration purposes only. Shops offered to you may pay more or less than the amounts suggested.*

Many times when you are reimbursed for a purchase that has value, you will receive only a small additional fee or no fee at all. For example, if you receive free meals, a hair cut, a vision examination, or other benefit, your fee may be small or nonexistent.

You will be told what fee you will receive and what the available reimbursement is when the shop is offered to you. You decide if it is worthwhile for you to do it. If a significant portion of the compensation is reimbursement based, and the required purchase is not of value to you, you might not want to do the shop.

As an example, your compensation for shopping a vision care provider might be a free eye exam, a discount on glasses or contact lenses, and a fee such as $10 or $20. If you don't need a vision examination or new glasses, it might not be worthwhile for you to do the shop just for the fee. On the other hand, if you are due for an eye exam, the value you receive could make this very attractive to you.

If a purchase is required, you will pay for it out of pocket and receive your reimbursement when you are paid for the shop. It can take a few days to several weeks to get paid, with three to six weeks being typical. Using a credit card to pay (if allowed) gives you more time before you have to come up with the cash. Many times, you will have your reimbursement from the mystery shopping company before you have to pay your credit card bill. Occasionally, you will receive gift certificates or vouchers to pay for some or all of your purchase, so you won't have to pay then wait for reimbursement.

Restaurant reimbursements may range from $5 or $10 for a fast food shop to $150, $200 or more for a fine dining shop. Many buffet or full service restaurants will reimburse $20 to $50. The reimbursement level is based on the cost of meals at that restaurant, and will usually cover reasonable costs for two people. You won't be paid more than you spend, so if the maximum reimbursement is $40 and you spend $38, you'll get $38. The guidelines will tell you if there are specific items you should or should not order, such as alcohol. Your reimbursement includes the tip in a full service restaurant or fine dining establishment.

Bar shops often reimburse a purchase of $20 to $50, and your purchase may include a snack or meal as well as one or two alcoholic beverages for the shopper and a companion.

Many retail shops don't include a purchase reimbursement. You may be asked to make a return of the item purchased and report on the return transaction.

Some retail shops include a token reimbursement, such as $2 to $5, so you can make a small purchase. However, others will include greater reimbursement or a significant discount on your purchase. For example, you might receive 50% of your purchase amount up to a set limit.

Shops that require a purchase of services or other intangibles, such as salons, movie theaters, dry cleaners, auto repair shops, etc. will reimburse for a specified purchase. For example, when shopping a salon you might be reimbursed for a shampoo, cut and style or blow dry, but not for getting your hair colored or permed. An oil change would be paid for when shopping an auto repair center, but not a tune-up or new brakes.

Don't assume that a purchase will be reimbursed. Always look at the shop guidelines. If it is not clear to you what will be paid for, ask.

When you receive a fee in addition to your purchase reimbursement it may range from $5 or $10 to $20, $50 or more. The amount of the fee will depend on factors such as how much time is required to do the shop and complete the report and if any special expertise or training is required. You may receive a bonus for doing a rush job when someone else canceled, or for doing a shop that is hard to assign.

Fees for fee-only shops start at about $10 for a very simple shop and may go up to $20, $50, $100 or more. The fee is usually based on how much time you must spend doing the shop, how simple or complex the report is, if any special expertise or experience is required, and the difficulty of finding shoppers to do the assignment. For example, the fee for a bank shop might be anywhere in the above range, depending on what is required of the shopper.

Fees for narrative reports or reports requiring extensive comments are usually higher than for reports which require you to complete a check-off form with just a few comments. Video shoppers often receive higher fees than shoppers doing standard written reports. Even though a video shopper usually doesn't have to write a report, the special expertise and training required to complete a quality video shop commands a higher fee.

The Bottom Line

Because assignments can be infrequent, you will not get rich as a mystery shopper. However, if you want to get an occasional free meal or free merchandise and make some extra cash while doing something enjoyable, mystery shopping is for you. Many shoppers have reported that with a little effort, and by being flexible about the types of assignments they accept, they often make hundreds of dollars a month in cash and free meals and merchandise as part time mystery shoppers.

In addition, mystery shoppers are sometimes offered other types of work. Many of the companies that will hire you to mystery shop also do market research, merchandising and other work for their clients. You may be asked if you would like these assignments, too. These might involve things such as stocking displays, counting merchandise in stock, and conducting customer surveys and exit interviews. Many of these assignments pay by the hour, not by the job. While you are never under any obligation to accept an assignment, these jobs can provide you with additional work and increase your income.

Can You Make a Living as a Mystery Shopper?

Most shoppers do this part time or spare time as a way of making extra money. There are a few mystery shopping companies that hire full time shoppers to handle all the shops in an area. Other companies don't offer full time work, but may have a lot of work for dependable shoppers in certain areas.

Most of the time, you won't be able to get enough work from one, two or even ten companies to keep you busy and make a full time income. There are shoppers who make a full time income by working with 50, 80, or more companies. They may not have assignments from each of those companies every month, but they are juggling assignments from many companies at the same time.

Making a full time income as a mystery shopper isn't easy. It takes tremendous organizational skills, and you have to be very motivated. You will have to be flexible about the types of shops you are willing to do. It helps to be open to accepting jobs other than mystery shops, such as audits and surveys or merchandising.

You also may have to flexible about how far you are willing to travel. One full time shopper said that she will accept assignments that may be 100 miles or more from her home. She lines up many shops to be done along the way, then spends the day driving along her route, doing all the scheduled shops. This shopper knows how much she needs to earn in a day to reach the income goal she has set for herself. She books shops that will pay her at least that much, plus cover her expenses (e.g., gas and other automobile costs, meals, etc.).

Full time mystery shopping is not realistic for the vast majority of mystery shoppers, but if you think you would like to shop full time, here are a few tips:

If you haven't mystery shopped before, apply to several companies and do some shops to be sure you enjoy the work and want to do it full time.

Contact the companies whose web sites say they hire full time shoppers and ask if there are openings in your area.

Get certified. Shoppers who are MSPA Gold Certified may be offered more and better assignments. Silver Certification is helpful, but if you want a large volume of assignments, you should "go for the Gold." For information on certification, go to http://www.mysteryshop.org/certification.php.

Apply to every mystery shopping company you can find. Let them know you are interested in a heavy volume of shops and you are willing to be flexible about your availability, types of shops, areas shopped, etc.

Stay in touch with the companies and schedulers you have worked for, and let them know you are interested in a heavier work load. If you have done a good job for them, and they have more work available, they will probably try to steer assignments your way.

As your work load increases, set up a good organization system to keep track of your assignments. Make sure you confirm offered assignments promptly, allow yourself plenty of time to do the shops you've accepted, and submit your reports promptly.

Although full time mystery shopping is not possible (or even desirable) for most shoppers, it can be done. Be prepared to work very hard, and you may be able to make it work for you.

Mystery Shoppers and Taxes

This section addresses taxation information under the United States' tax code. If you are not subject to U.S. tax laws, consult your taxing authority to determine how your mystery shopping income will be handled.

When mystery shopping, you will most often work as an independent contractor. That means that the companies paying you don't withhold income taxes, Social Security taxes or Medicare taxes. *You* are responsible for making sure your taxes are paid. In general, the fees you receive for mystery shopping are taxable as ordinary income, and are subject to federal income taxes, state and local income taxes, Social Security taxes, and Medicare taxes.

The good news is that when you are a contractor you are treated as a small business and you can deduct certain expenses. These may include postage, mileage and car expenses, travel, office equipment, computer and Internet fees, and perhaps even some purchases made while you are mystery shopping. You might qualify to deduct some of your housing expenses if you have a home office.

If any of the companies you work for pay you at least $600 during a year, they are required to provide you with a 1099 form. This is similar to the W2 form you would receive from an employer, and you will receive it at the same time (i.e., January of the following year). The information on the 1099 is also reported to the Internal Revenue Service, so if you don't account for the income you will hear from the IRS.

Companies that did not pay you at least $600 are not required to send a 1099 form, and they may not report to the IRS how much they paid you. Many mystery shoppers mistakenly believe this means they don't have to pay taxes on that income, so they don't report it. However, the income is taxable, and must be accounted for. You should have the integrity to do so, but you should also know that it can be discovered. For example, if the mystery shopping company is audited, tax auditors may verify that the money they say was paid to contractors was reported on the contractors' tax returns.

To report your independent contractor income, you will file a Schedule C with your regular tax return. For instructions on record keeping, what expenses you may deduct, and how to complete Schedule C, contact the IRS and ask for their publications on small business taxes. You can often find these publications at your local library, or they can be downloaded at the IRS web site. The IRS also offers free workshops and an online course for sole proprietors. See the small business area of the IRS web site at http://www.irs.gov/ for more information.

You may be required to file quarterly estimated taxes if you make a significant income as a shopper or from other independent contractor activities, and you don't have other income which is subject to withholding. If you or your spouse are employed full time and have taxes withheld from your income, and mystery shopping represents a small part of your income, this probably won't be an issue for you. For more information, call your local IRS office and ask for information about quarterly estimated taxes, or search for "quarterly estimated taxes" at the IRS web site.

Tax regulations are always changing, so be sure to refer to IRS publications, their web site and other guides for current tax information. You may want to consult your tax preparer for additional information about how your mystery shopping income and expenses should be reported.

For more information on tax issues, go to the IRS web site at http://www.irs.gov/.

Canadian Tax Issues

Laws in Canada are somewhat different. For example, Canadian companies do not provide anything comparable to the 1099 required of U.S. companies. However, the taxability of income and deductibility of expenses under Canadian law is similar to the U.S.

For information about Canadian tax law, visit the Canada Revenue Agency web site: http://cra-arc.gc.ca/.

International Shoppers

Shoppers outside of the U.S. and Canada, or those who shop across international borders, should contact the taxing authorities in their home countries to determine how their income will be taxed.

Being an Independent Contractor

Most mystery shoppers are independent contractors, not employees. What's the difference? As an independent contractor, you are treated as a small business. This has both advantages and disadvantages to you.

When you are an employee, the employer is responsible for withholding income taxes from your pay, and matching your Social Security (FICA) and Medicare taxes. As an independent contractor, you receive the full amount of your pay and you are responsible for paying any taxes due. You may be required to file quarterly estimated income tax returns. Independent contractors are usually not covered by unemployment and workers compensation laws, so are not eligible for benefits.

The good news is that you get many of the tax breaks available to businesses, because you are now a small business person. For example, you can deduct expenses you incur in earning your income, such as computers, Internet access, cell phones, education, postage, phone calls, etc. (Although you can't take a deduction if you were reimbursed by the mystery shopping company.) You can take a tax deduction for a mileage allowance or a portion of your total car expenses. You may be able to deduct a portion of your housing costs as a home office.

Nevada Shoppers

Nevada has the most stringent mystery shopping laws. Under current law, mystery shopping can only be performed by licensed private investigators. To mystery shop in Nevada, you must be an employee of a licensed private investigator. Independent contractors are not used. Because you are an employee, some companies will want you to work for them exclusively, while others will be open to you working for other companies.

To become a mystery shopper in Nevada, apply to a company that has the proper Nevada licensing. Two such companies are:

Howard Services/Service Sleuths
http://www.servicesleuths.com/

QSI Specialists
http://www.globalintelligence.net/

If they have a need for shoppers, they will contact you. If you are accepted, you will be asked to apply for a work card. This includes having a background check done. You will generally have to pay this fee.

The mystery shopping company/private investigator will register you with the state as their employee. They will generally pay the registration fee for this.

Independent Contractor Agreements

Who decides whether you are an employee or an independent contractor? The Internal Revenue Service has a set of guidelines that can be used to make that determination. The guidelines are subject to change, but indications that a worker is a contractor rather than an employee include when the worker:

> is paid by the job, not by the hour;
> set his or her own work hours;
> performs similar services for other persons or companies;
> furnishes his or her own materials, supplies and equipment;
> can realize a profit or loss; and
> can choose to accept or reject a job assignment.

As an independent contractor you will be asked to sign a contractor agreement. The agreement will include specific mention of many of these conditions. Don't panic if, for example, the agreement says that you understand you may make a profit or suffer a loss. It is highly unlikely that you will lose money working as a contract mystery shopper. The language is in the agreement to comply with IRS guidelines about independent contractors.

As an independent contractor, you are free to offer your services to anyone. Having business cards is evidence of the fact that you are offering your services to many companies. When you have business cards, mystery shopping companies see it as evidence that you take your shopping career seriously and you treat it as a business. See page 64 for tips on creating and using business cards.

Standard provisions in an independent contractor agreement include that no employment relationship is established; that the company does not guarantee any minimum amount of work and you are not required to accept any assignment; and that the agreement may be terminated by either party at any time.

Many of the agreements you are asked to sign will contain similar provisions and language, but read each one carefully and keep a copy for yourself. It is a legal agreement and you can and will be held to its terms.

If you see a provision in a contractor agreement that makes you uncomfortable, don't agree to it. You may want to ask for clarification from the mystery shopping company or an attorney before signing. Of course, you can always refuse to sign an agreement. If you do so you won't be eligible for assignments from that company, but there are lots of other companies you can work with.

Instead of signing a physical piece of paper, you may become contracted by reading the agreement online, then clicking a button that says "I agree." Treat this as if you were actually signing the agreement. Read it carefully, print a copy, then click on "I agree."

Confidentiality and Non-Compete Clauses

The independent contractor agreement will usually address confidentiality. As a mystery shopper, you have access to confidential and proprietary information about the mystery shopping company and its clients. The company could suffer financial loss or damage to its client relationships if you were to divulge this information, so you are required to agree to keep all dealings with the company and its clients confidential.

This means that at a minimum you shouldn't talk to others about specific mystery shopping assignments you've done, you should never share report forms, completed reports, manuals or other materials with others, and you shouldn't talk about clients or compensation schedules of the mystery shopping company.

Some companies will include a non-compete clause in the agreement. This clause says that while you work for them, and for a specified period thereafter (usually one year), you agree not to enter into a mystery shopping or evaluation business.

The clause will probably be written to allow you to work for other mystery shopping companies. It is designed to prohibit you from starting your own business and going into competition against the mystery shopping company. Don't agree to this if you plan to start your own mystery shopping company. You may not take it seriously, but they do.

Working with More than One Company

Even if you are an excellent worker and make yourself available 24 hours a day, you won't necessarily get as many assignments as you would like from one company. A lot depends on how many clients the shopping company has in your area, how often they are shopped, and how many other shoppers are competing for these shops.

To get more work, you should apply to more companies. Most companies will ask if you have ever worked as a shopper, and they won't care if you are currently working for someone else. These companies understand that the work they have to offer is sporadic, and they won't fault you for trying to get more work than they can offer.

When the application asks for what other mystery shopping companies you have worked, it does not violate your independent contractor agreements to list the names of mystery shopping companies. You should not name specific clients you've shopped, but it is fine to name the mystery shopping companies.

Ethics

That brings us to the ethics of working for more than one company. While there is nothing wrong with accepting assignments from several companies, you must respect the confidentiality of the information you receive from each company.

Pay attention to the terms of the confidentiality agreements, or confidentiality clauses of independent contractor agreements, you signed when you applied. At a minimum, follow these guidelines:

Don't share information with anyone about a mystery shopping company's clients, or shops you have done for any mystery shopping company.

Don't disclose the names of companies that have mystery shopping programs. Many shoppers believe that it is acceptable to post comments or questions about clients or shops to public forums, as long as they don't disclose which mystery shopping company has that client. It is not.

Don't send copies of blank report forms, sample reports, or completed reports from one company to another.

Don't share information about compensation with other mystery shopping companies, clients or other shoppers.

If a friend asks for advice about becoming a mystery shopper, you may refer them to mystery shopping companies you recommend, but don't disclose information about the clients they shop, fees and reimbursements, etc.

Don't give educational materials or other documents you received from one company to another.

Don't gossip about the people or clients of any of the companies you work with.

Don't discuss the results of mystery shops directly with the client, unless you have been asked to do so by the mystery shopping company.

Don't post proprietary information about a mystery shopping company or client to an Internet message board, chat or forum.

If you are not sure whether it is ethical to divulge something you know, DON'T DO IT! It is always better to be safe than sorry.

Remember that this is a business and you are a professional. Take your responsibilities seriously.

Business Card Tips

Include your name, e-mail address, phone number(s) and where you shop.

You may also include your certification status, and a title such as mystery shopper, customer service evaluator, etc.

Cards can be printed in small quantities on your computer printer, or they can be ordered from your local office supply store or print shop, or from one of many online printers, such as http://www.vistaprint.com/.

Where to use your business cards: at shopper get-togethers when you are networking with fellow shoppers, when you meet mystery shopping company representatives at industry functions such as certification or conferences, and when you mail anything to a company.

Don't drop cards saying you are a mystery shopper into drawings at restaurants and other businesses.

How to Get Started

Most of the time, mystery shoppers are hired by companies that specialize in performing mystery shops, not directly by the businesses that are mystery shopped. Because you'll work for mystery shopping companies that serve many different clients, you may have the opportunity to evaluate businesses of all kinds. You'll find an extensive list of companies that hire mystery shoppers in Appendix A of this book. The companies listed have online applications and you should apply online.

Some companies (especially local or regional companies) may not be set up to take your application online and would prefer to receive a resume and letter of interest. However, if a mystery shopping company has an online application you should assume that is how they prefer to be contacted

In general, most mystery shopping companies do not want you to call. They are managing hundreds or thousands of shops and shoppers during a single month, and they don't have a lot of time to spend on the phone. Of course, they encourage you to e-mail or call if you have questions about an assignment, but don't call to ask if they got your application, or when they will have an assignment for you. If they need you, they will be in touch.

Keep track of the companies to which you've applied. You may think you will remember all of the applications you submitted, but you won't. Don't waste your time by submitting multiple applications to the same companies. Each of the company listings in Appendix A has space for you to make notes about the applications you have submitted.

Don't Pay a Fee to Apply

Reputable mystery shopping companies will not charge an application fee. Do not pay a fee to submit your application or to be entered into a database of shoppers.

Companies asking you to pay are often not even mystery shopping companies. There is no guarantee that you will get assignments by paying the fee.

There are hundreds of companies to which you can apply without paying a fee. Save your money by skipping any that expect you to pay.

Applying Online

In every area of mystery shopping, including the application, each company has its own policies and procedures. What is true one place is not necessarily true at another. That means that it is always important to read any instructions you are given, starting with how to complete the application.

The primary reason that mystery shopping companies reject applicants is that they did not fully complete the application. Answer every question. If you are asked for a writing sample, provide it. Companies told me that as many as 20% to 25% of applicants don't make it through the first screening because they did not provide all of the information required.

When you apply for a job, there are restrictions regarding the types of questions employers can ask prior to hiring you. Because we are all used to those limitations, some of the questions asked on a mystery shopping application for independent contractors may seem odd or inappropriate. You may be asked your age, race, marital status, number of children and their ages, if you own a car, if you have pets, whether you wear glasses, etc. Some companies may make these questions optional, while others will require that you answer to be considered for shops.

The good news is that questions such as these are not asked in order to *exclude* you, they are asked in order to *include* you. Some assignments require shoppers to be over or under a certain age to match the demographics of the client's customers. They may need three couples each of a different race or ethnicity to test compliance with non-discrimination laws. Shoppers may have to be accompanied by children. If someone is going to mystery shop a pet grooming service, they need a pet.

You might be concerned about providing personal information, including your Social Security Number, over the Internet. It is unlikely that someone is going to intercept your data transmission, and most companies use a secure server, which encrypts the data, for greater security. The company may need your Social Security Number for tax reasons. If you refuse to provide it, some companies will automatically reject your application.

One way to tell if the company uses a secure server is that the URL will begin with "https://" instead of "http://." If the server is not secure and you wish to apply, enter a dummy number, such as all 9's, then e-mail the company to let them know that you will provide the Social Security Number by fax or postal mail.

How do you know you can trust the company asking for the information? One big clue is whether the company is a member of the Mystery Shopping Providers Association (MSPA). Members are required to operate according to the Association's professional standards and ethics. You can verify whether a company belongs at the MSPA's web site:

http://www.mysteryshop.org/. Members also may display the MSPA logo on their web sites.

Belonging to the MSPA is a sign that a company is honest, ethical and professional, but not belonging doesn't mean that the company is not a good one. If you run across a company that is not a member, spend a little time looking around their web site. Does the site appear to be professional? Is there information about the company and its owners? What does the web site say about how the company operates? If you don't have a good feeling about the company, don't apply. Just go on to the next one.

Completing the Application

Remember that a big part of your responsibility as a mystery shopper is filling out report forms and writing comments and narratives. If you don't bother to do a good job on the application, why should they believe that you will be thorough and accurate in completing your reports?

Spelling, grammar and punctuation matter. When providing a writing sample, create it in your word processor and make sure you spell check it. Then cut and paste the sample into the application. Of course, you should carefully proofread all of your application to catch any mistakes. Some companies are more forgiving than others on these matters, but why handicap yourself by doing a less-than-excellent job?

Don't fill out the application in ALL CAPS or all lower case. Your keyboard has a shift key, so use it to properly capitalize the first word in each sentence, proper nouns, etc. Many people get sloppy when writing on the computer and drop letters, ignore punctuation, use abbreviations such as "u" for "you," and otherwise make mistakes which are not acceptable in a mystery shopping report. Don't do these things on your application, either.

Some companies with online applications will ask you to print and mail a copy of their Independent Contractor agreement, or they will ask for a handwriting sample or other documentation. If they request it, do it. And do it promptly. If you take weeks to do something simple like print, sign and mail a contract, how long will it take you to complete an assignment?

Tests and Quizzes

As a part of the screening process, you may be tested. These tests may be on general subjects, such as your ability to read and follow directions or spelling and grammar issues, or they may be specific to client requirements. For example, you might be asked to review the shop guidelines and then answer a series of questions about completing the shop.

Companies that require testing will not assign shops to you until you have successfully completed the tests. Don't be nervous about taking a test, but take your time. Prepare by reading any material you are given, then read each question and all possible answers carefully before answering.

Applying by Phone or Mail

A few companies will ask for only basic information online, then mail an application packet for you to complete. Companies without an online application may want you to call or write for an application packet. If a company doesn't have a web site, a good way to apply to them is to send a one-page resume and one-page letter of interest (see examples starting on page 74) through the mail. Always include a self-addressed, stamped envelope when you send a resume to a mystery shopping company. It makes it easier for them to respond with a letter or application.

When they send an application packet, it may include an application, a demographic information form (where you give information about your age, marital status, etc.), an Independent Contractor agreement, and a sample shop form. The company may also include information about the types of shops they do, their standards, when and how you can expect to be paid, etc.

When you receive an application packet be sure to complete all forms and return them quickly, along with anything else they request, such as a photo or a handwriting sample. They keep track of when they sent it and when it was returned. If you take weeks or months to complete the application, it doesn't bode well for how you'll do on a shop.

Resume and Letter of Interest

If the entire application process is online, you won't need to send a resume. However, sending a resume and letter of interest is a good way to approach companies that don't have an online application.

Even if you make all of your applications online and never need to send a paper resume, writing one is a useful exercise. The process gets you to focus on what your qualifications are, and when you are done you have the information you need to fill out your applications on one handy page.

Show that you are a professional. Type (or computer generate) your resume and cover letter (unless they specify handwritten). Don't use hot pink paper. Your resume should be on white, beige or light gray paper.

One mystery shopping company told me they received a letter written on notebook paper in crayon! Maybe the writer thought it was a good way to make his letter stand out and get attention. Well, his letter did stand out, and he did get attention. What he didn't get was a job. Be a pro.

On the following pages you'll find samples of a resume and letter of interest. Yours shouldn't look exactly like these, of course, but they are provided as examples of the kind of information that should be included. Make your resume and cover letter reflect your experience and qualifications.

Remember that mystery shopping companies need to know where you can shop, when you can shop, a little about your background, and enough personal demographic information that the company can match you to shops (e.g., tell them if you are married, have kids, wear glasses, own a car, own pets, have hobbies, etc.). Many companies use zip codes to assign shops, so let them know what zip codes you are willing to shop in. You might list anywhere from three to ten zip codes on your resume or in your letter of interest. (Many of the online applications you complete will ask for zip codes, too.)

Keep your resume and cover letter to one page each. You don't need to list every job you ever had, but tell where you are currently working and describe your background.

Mystery shoppers can be male or female, young moms or "seasoned citizens", employed, self-employed, homemakers or retirees. You don't need a college degree or special training and experience. So whoever you are, put your resume together to put your best foot forward and get started now!

Sample Resume

Merry Shopper
123 Main Street
Anytown, USA 23456
(123) 456-7890/(123) 456-7891 Fax
merry@shop.com

- Experienced mystery shopper
- Extensive background in customer service
- [X] years' experience in [retail/hospitality/etc.]
- Excellent written and verbal communication skills
- Proficient in use of the personal computer, including Microsoft Word, Excel, Access and other programs.
- Reliable transportation
- Flexible availability - days, evenings and weekends
- Accessible by phone/voice mail, pager/cell phone
- Own a computer with e-mail and Internet access
- Fax capabilities (send and receive) at home

Work History

[Provide your current employer's name and a brief description of your duties. You may list previous employers or provide a few sentences about your background. If you haven't worked outside the home for several years, your experience as a homemaker may be relevant.]

Educational Achievements

[Do you have a degree? Have you taken courses or seminars in customer service, marketing, or writing?]

Personal Information

[Normally, it is not a good idea to list personal information on a resume. However, it could work *for* you as a mystery shopper. Mention if you are married, have children or pets, wear glasses, own a car, etc. This could qualify you for assignments with special requirements.]

Sample Letter of Interest

Merry Shopper
123 Main Street
Anytown, USA 23456
(123) 456-7890 / (123) 456-7891 Fax
merry@shop.com

Dear Sir or Madam:

I am an experienced mystery shopper and I wish to apply to be a contract mystery shopper with your company. My resume is enclosed.

I have a flexible schedule which allows me to complete assignments days or evenings, weekdays or weekends. I have reliable transportation, and own a fax machine and a personal computer with full Internet access. My husband is sometimes available for assignments requiring a couple, and I am a pet owner.

Anytown is in the Houston metropolitan area. I am available for assignments in zip codes 23456, 23460, 23277, 23480 and 23478.

My work experience includes many years in technical and management positions requiring excellent communication skills. I also have several years' experience in retail and food service, including a position as Assistant Manager of a fast food outlet.

Thank you for considering my application. I can be contacted at the above number during day or evening hours. There is an answering machine to take messages if I am unavailable. My mobile phone number is 123-456-7897.

I look forward to hearing from you!

Sincerely yours,

Merry Shopper

TIP:

When applying online, print copies of the completed application, independent contractor agreement, and company information from each web site where you apply.

This is an easy way to keep a record of the companies to which you've applied and the terms of your agreements with the companies.

Quick-Start Plan

Follow these steps to jump start your mystery shopping career. This plan is designed to get you started efficiently and easily, and it helps you avoid mistakes that could cost you time and money, now and in the future.

Choose an e-mail address you will use for all of your mystery shopping communications.
This may be your usual e-mail address, or you may choose to establish a new address, just to be used for mystery shopping. Make sure it is an address that you expect to have for a long time. If your e-mail address changes, you will have to update your records at all of the mystery shopping companies to which you have applied.

If your e-mail address is through your ISP (the service you use to get to the Internet, such as AOL), then it will change when you change ISPs. Free e-mail accounts, such as Yahoo, Hotmail and others, can be used no matter what service you use to access the Internet; however, they may have limitations regarding the number of e-mails you can receive, the size of attachments, etc.

My e-mail address is cathy@idealady.com. I own the IdeaLady.com domain, so I will always be able to receive e-mails at that address. If you have a web site, you may wish to use one of your e-mail addresses at that web site for mystery shopping.

Get a PayPal account.
PayPal is an online payment service that many mystery shopping companies are now using to pay shoppers. In fact, in order to work for some companies you must have a PayPal account and be willing to accept payment through them.

Your PayPal account is free. Simply go to http://www.paypal.com/ and sign up. Make sure that the e-mail address you plan to use for mystery shopping is associated with your PayPal account. That is how the payments from mystery shopping companies will get to your PayPal account.

When a payment is sent to you, you will get an e-mail stating that you have a payment from the mystery shopping company. There are several ways to get the money from your PayPal account. You can have it sent by direct deposit to a bank account, ask for a check, spend it with a PayPal debit card, or use it to make online purchases from merchants who accept PayPal. For example, many eBay sellers accept PayPal payments.

Get certified.

This is a good time to complete the MSPA Silver Certification. Do it before you start submitting applications, and you can enter your certification code when you apply. That way, you won't have to go back and update all of your records. Also consider obtaining your Gold Certification as soon as you can.

Silver Certification can be completed online at http://www.mysteryshop.org/certification.php.

Prepare to apply.

Put together a sheet with all of the information you will need to complete the online applications, such as your education and employment history. Many applications will also ask where you are willing to shop. Prepare a list of cities and towns, zip codes or area codes where you are willing to accept assignments.

Prepare your writing samples.

Many applications will ask for a paragraph on one or more of the following: an example of a good customer experience, an example of a poor customer experience, and why you want to be a mystery shopper or why you believe you would make a good mystery shopper.

These writing samples are important, so it is worthwhile to make sure they reflect well on you.

Companies use the writing samples to evaluate your writing skills. Do the samples show that you use proper spelling, grammar and punctuation? They also look at what you write. Look at the section of this book on writing comments and narratives for specific examples of what companies like and what they don't like. Make your writing samples objective and specific. Include details. And don't "trash" anyone. Even if the service was poor, your report should not be an attack. Just state the facts.

Start applying to companies.
Use the list in Appendix A to get started. You can also search for companies by geographic area or by the industries they shop by going to the MSPA web site, http://www.mysteryshop.org/shoppers.php.

You should apply to many companies in order to make yourself available for the most shopping opportunities. By following the steps outlined above, you should be able to complete several applications in a short period of time. Then, take a few minutes every day or a few times a week to fill out another application or two.

Make sure you apply to scheduling companies. These companies schedule shops for many different mystery shopping companies, and they usually schedule a high volume of shops. Scheduling companies include:

Kern Scheduling Services
http://www.kernscheduling.com/

Coast to Coast Scheduling Services
http://www.ctcss.com/

BLD Scheduling
http://www.BLDSchedulers.com/

When you submit an application at the Archon Development web site <http://www.archondev.com/>, your information is forwarded to the more than 50 mystery shopping companies that use the Prophet system created by Archon.

Pay attention to how the companies schedule.
When you apply to each company, they will generally tell you how they schedule shops. Some will send e-mails announcing when they have shops in your area, others want you to check back at their web sites to watch for postings. They will usually tell you when they expect to post new shops and how you can get assignments. Make a note of how shops are assigned by each company, then follow the steps they outline to apply for the assignments you want.

Visit job boards and watch your e-mail to get assignments.

After applying you will start receiving e-mail notices of shop opportunities, and you should visit companies' job boards to check for available assignments.

Make sure your spam filters are not blocking e-mails from mystery shopping companies. Because these e-mails are typically sent in bulk, some e-mail systems will erroneously consider them spam.

When you get your first assignment, do a great job.

Your first assignments probably won't be glamorous, but they will get you in the door. Take them seriously and do a great job in order to get more assignments from that company. As you gain experience, you will get the opportunity to do more assignments including those with higher pay and reimbursements.

International Mystery Shopping

Mystery shopping is done around the world. Although this book is written from the perspective of mystery shopping in the United States and Canada, the issues addressed by mystery shopping are much the same around the world.

If you are a U.S.-based shopper wishing to shop internationally, you should apply to U.S. companies that shop internationally. Don't assume if you are going to Europe that you will be able to get assignments from mystery shopping companies located there.

Many U.S. shoppers who shop internationally work in the travel industry or for airlines. They often travel abroad and mystery shopping companies can establish relationships with them and use them repeatedly.

Familiarity with etiquette and local customs, including tipping standards, is a big plus. And it is helpful to have a high limit credit card available to charge your expenses.

U.S. companies that shop internationally include:

Bare Associates International
http://www.baiservices.com/

Coast to Coast Scheduling Services
http://www.ctcss.com/

International Shoppers

If you are a shopper located outside the United States, you should apply to companies located in your home country and neighboring areas.

You will find a list of companies located around the world in the International section of the mystery shopping company directory in Appendix A of this book. You can locate additional companies by doing an online search for "mystery shopping" and your country name. Find more international companies at:

Mystery Shopping Providers Association
http://www.mysteryshop.org/europe/shoppers
.php

Volition.com
http://www.volition.com/mysteryint.html

Types of Mystery Shops

Mystery shopping can take many forms. Here are some common types of shops:

Traditional Mystery Shop
A traditional mystery shop involves visiting the business as a customer, then completing an evaluation form or narrative describing the customer service, cleanliness, quality, sales skills, and other aspects of the experience.

Reveal Shop
In a reveal shop, also known as a reward shop, if an employee meets certain performance criteria, the mystery shopper identifies him/herself as the mystery shopper and presents an award (e.g., gift certificate or other prize) to the employee. The shopper may also be required to notify a manager if the employee does not qualify for the reward.

Competitive Shop

This is similar to a traditional shop, but it is used to compare the performance of a client's location to one or more of their competitors. The shopper usually uses the same report form that is used to shop the client.

Pricing Audit

During pricing audits, the shopper discreetly notes the prices of certain items. This may be done as a type of competitive shop, or the audit may be performed on behalf of a vendor or supplier.

Telephone Shop

This may be a part of a traditional mystery shop, or a stand-alone shop. It involves calling the client location to evaluate service and compliance with standards and procedures.

The shopper may complete a written report form describing what happened during the call, or the call may be recorded and the recording given to the client.

Audio and Video Shops

The shopper records interactions with the client's employees using a hidden audio or video recorder. Some states have laws governing the use of recording devices, so be aware of the laws in your state. One source for information is the Reporters Committee for Freedom of the Press at http://rcfp.org/taping.

Digital Photo Shops
These shops require that the shopper use a digital camera to take photos of products, displays, signage, or other areas. Photos may be taken discreetly or with the knowledge of the employees, depending on the assignment.

Internet Service Evaluation
In these online shops, also known as cyber shops, the shopper may make an online purchase, or ask a question via e-mail, to evaluate the ease of ordering or customer service responsiveness. Internet service evaluations may be used by retailers, travel companies, florists, and other online businesses. In some cases, the shopper may be asked to place an order online, pick up the purchase at a retail location, then return the item.

Integrity Shops
In an integrity shop, the shopper may be asked to verify that cash handling procedures are being followed, or even test an employee to determine if they are behaving honestly. The nature of these shops means that they may be subject to regulations, such as requiring that you work for a private investigator. For information about private investigator laws, see the CrimeTime web site at http://www.crimetime.com/licensing.htm.

Getting Assignments

Once your application has been accepted and your information has been entered into a mystery shopping company's database, you are eligible to start receiving assignments. You may receive an assignment very soon after applying, or it may be three to six weeks or longer before you get your first mystery shopping opportunity. The time required to get your first assignments depends on the number of companies to which you apply, the number of shoppers and available assignments in your area, how often you check your e-mail and job boards, and other factors, including luck. Many companies schedule the bulk of their shops once a month, but shops are scheduled all through the month due to cancellations and new projects.

Don't expect to receive a lot of assignments right away. Some companies will never contact you because they simply won't have assignments available in your area. Others may be happy to send you all the work they can once they know that you can be depended on to do a good job, but they will probably only offer one or two assignments to begin. Companies will not start you out with a lot of assignments because they want to make sure that you will do your assignments and that you will do a good job with them before increasing your work load.

You might be surprised to learn that an average of 25% of assignments accepted by shoppers are not completed. That means that the company has to find another shopper to complete the assignment, often at the last-minute, 25% of the time. In fact, it happens so often companies even have a word for it: flaking. If you hear that someone flaked on a shop that means that they didn't do the shop and either canceled at the last minute or never even let the company know they weren't going to do the shop. They just disappeared.

In a perfect world, you would know exactly which companies need shoppers in your area and you could focus your efforts on those companies. You will find that some companies list at their web sites the places they are actively seeking shoppers. However, that is always subject to change. A company may get a new client with locations in your town, or lose a client with a presence in your town. That will affect their need for shoppers.

Although most companies give preference to their proven shoppers, they also need to bring in new shoppers on a regular basis. To increase your chances of being offered assignments you should make your application the best it can be, follow all directions when applying for shops, and be flexible. Often, your first opportunity with a new company will come because another shopper flaked and someone is needed to complete an assignment as soon as possible. Even if it's a little bit inconvenient to do so, accepting such a shop will get you in the door and in the good graces of the scheduler you helped out. Another key to getting assignments with a new company is MSPA certification. Many MSPA member companies give priority to Silver and Gold Certified shoppers when scheduling shops.

What if you applied several weeks or months ago, and have never gotten an assignment? It probably means that they don't have a need for shoppers in your area right now. Should you contact them? Probably not. However, if you haven't heard from them in several months it is acceptable to send a brief e-mail letting them know that you are still interested in shopping for them. Be sure to include your identifying information: name, address, phone number, where you are willing to shop, etc.

Notify the companies you applied to if your information changes. For example, if your name changes due to marriage or divorce, you move, you get a new phone number or area code, your e-mail address changes, or your employment status or availability changes you should notify the companies to which you applied. Most companies don't want you to fill out a completely new application when this happens. You may be able to notify them by e-mail or fill out an update form on the web. Check the company web sites to see how they prefer to receive updates.

How Shops Are Scheduled

Companies schedule assignments many different ways, including via the Internet, message boards, e-mail, and telephone. A single company may use more than one method of scheduling shops.

Scheduling via Web Sites

Some companies want you to check their web site regularly and claim any shops you want to do. This is known as "self-assigning" or "self-scheduling." They may tell you what dates the site will list new shops, or they may send e-mail to let you know that new shops have been added. It is your responsibility to check the web site and notify the company that you would like to do a shop.

The web site will have the specifics of the shop, such as the deadline, the client or type of shop, the fee and any reimbursement to be paid. You may also be able to review all guidelines and forms associated with the shop before you choose to accept it.

These assignments are usually first-come, first-served, so you need to check the site right away to claim shops. However, self-assigning is not as random as it may appear. Most companies that use self-assigning have a screening mechanism in place. When you log in to the web site you will see only the shops for which you are eligible. If there are special requirements, such as demographic requirements or experience level, you will only see the shop as available if you meet those requirements. For example, many shops have rotation requirements. This might mean that the same shopper can only visit that location once every 90 days. If you were assigned that location last month, you would not be eligible and the shop would not appear on your available shop list.

The trend in the mystery shopping industry is toward more automation, and you will see more companies using self-assignment in the future. As technology becomes more advanced it is possible to select shoppers with greater precision using such automated systems. Some companies may allow experienced and/or certified shoppers to self-assign, while other shoppers must apply and be assigned by a scheduler.

Scheduling via Job Boards

There are several job boards on the Internet where mystery shopping companies and schedulers post available shops. Interested shoppers are asked to register at a web site or send e-mail.

See the Internet Resources in Appendix C for information on accessing job boards. You can also find shop postings at the MSPA web site at http://www.mysteryshop.org/shoppers.php.

Scheduling via E-mail

Mystery shopping companies and schedulers often send e-mail to let shoppers know they have assignments available. For example, an e-mail might be sent to all of the shoppers in Louisiana to let them know about available shops in the state.

The e-mail will give the details of the shop, such as location, type of shop, due date, fees and reimbursements, etc. E-mail is often used to reschedule shops that were canceled by another shopper, so they may be rush jobs. In that case, a bonus or incentive may be offered to get the job done quickly.

If the e-mail was sent to reschedule a shop canceled by another shopper, the scheduler may need to assign the shop quickly. Checking your e-mail often can pay off in these cases.

When broadcast e-mails are used to notify shoppers of upcoming shops, the shops are not typically awarded on a first-come, first-served basis. Instead the scheduler may wait 24 to 48 hours, then review the applications received and decide which shopper is best for the assignment.

When making assignments, schedulers look at many criteria. The client may have specific requirements for the shopper, such as age, gender, or other demographic factors. Schedulers like to award assignments to shoppers who have proven themselves to be reliable, so they will consider the shopper's previous experience with them. How many shops have they completed and what was the quality of their reports? Has the shopper canceled assignments in the past? Or has the shopper stepped in to help out when someone else canceled? Are there any rotation requirements that must be addressed? And many companies will consider the shopper's certification status.

You may see repeated e-mails for some shops, because schedulers have a difficult time finding shoppers for certain locations. In other cases, they will receive 50, 100 or more applications for one particular shop. Don't take it personally when you don't receive a shop for which you have applied.

Scheduling via Telephone

Telephone scheduling may be used when a company needs to find a replacement shopper quickly for someone who has canceled. Or, you may receive your first assignment from a company by phone, so that they can talk with you before assigning the shop. Telephone scheduling isn't done often, but some shops are still scheduled over the phone.

What to Do When Contacted

Whenever you are contacted by a mystery shopping company, follow their instructions. You generally aren't expected to respond to an e-mail that is sent to all of the shoppers in an area announcing a shop, unless you want to be considered for the shop. However, if an e-mail is sent specifically to you offering a shop, respond as soon as possible.

The same thing goes for any other contact. If you are called about a shop, you are expected to respond quickly. Never let it go more than 24 hours, and respond sooner if you can.

Once You're Confirmed

When you have accepted a shop and been confirmed, the mystery shopping company will send you detailed guidelines for completing the shop. They may fax, e-mail or mail forms, guidelines and sample reports to you. If the report is to be completed online, you'll be told where to log in to get your instructions and submit your report.

Working with Schedulers

In addition to working with schedulers who are on staff at a mystery shopping company, you may receive assignments from independent schedulers. These are contractors hired to assign the shops and make sure they are completed.

From a mystery shopper's perspective, working with independent schedulers is about the same as working directly with the mystery shopping company's schedulers. The advantage of working with these independent schedulers is that they may work with several mystery shopping companies. They use the database of shoppers who have applied to the mystery shopping company, as well as their own databases of shoppers.

By working with schedulers, you may get shops from companies you have never worked with or applied to before. And, just like the staff schedulers at mystery shopping companies, if an independent scheduler knows that she can count on you to do a good job, she will send shops your way when she can.

You can find schedulers in the Mystery Shopping Directory in Appendix A and in the Quick-Start Plan.

Getting More Shops

Here are some ways to increase the number of opportunities offered to you:

> Apply to many companies. You never know where your next job—or your best job—will come from.

When you complete an assignment, send your scheduler a brief thank you e-mail and let her know you would like to be considered for additional assignments.

Check job boards and your e-mail frequently. Follow-up promptly when you see a posting for an assignment you'd like.

Be open to trying something new. If you've never done a digital camera shop or shopped a bank, give it a try. You might like it!

Consider assignments other than mystery shopping. You might be offered opportunities for merchandising, audits, demos, surveys, exit interviews and other tasks. Often this type of work is scheduled by the same companies that offer mystery shops.

And, of course, always do a great job. When you do a great job companies will want to work with you again and again.

Other Opportunities for Mystery Shoppers

There are several other types of work that may appeal to mystery shoppers. Once you contract with mystery shopping companies, you may be offered opportunities to do other kinds of work for them.

In the Mystery Shopping Directory in Appendix A of this book you will find several companies that hire contractors for these types of jobs as well as mystery shopping

Merchandising

When you get one of these assignments, you will typically be working for a manufacturer or distributor rather than the retailer. It may involve going to a store and checking inventory to see if stock is low and the store needs to place an order for more. You may be asked to deliver an order and put it on the shelves. Sometimes you will set up a display and stock it. Or, just check a display and make sure it is neat and organized.

You may be asked to verify how merchandise is priced and displayed, including signage and what other products are nearby. Unlike when you are mystery shopping, you will identify yourself to store personnel. You may need to get a manager's signature to authorize an order, or to verify that you were in the store.

Merchandisers are often paid by the hour, but may be paid by the assignment. Some assignments will include a reimbursement for mileage. Just as with mystery shopping assignments, you are free to accept or reject any of these offers.

For more information and to locate merchandising jobs, visit the National Association for Retail Marketing Services at http://www.narms.com/. You may submit a profile (application) at the site that will be sent to more than 250 companies and stored in a searchable database at the NARMS site.

Pricing Audits

When performing pricing audits you enter a business and note the prices for certain items. This might involve going in to a fast food restaurant and getting prices for several menu items, or doing a detailed survey of prices in a grocery store.

These audits are often done on behalf of a competitor of the business you are auditing so, as with mystery shopping, you don't announce your presence and should gather your information discreetly.

Market Research

Many of the companies that do mystery shopping also do other types of market research, so you may be offered opportunities to conduct surveys as a market researcher or participate in market research studies.

This might include interviewing people over the phone or in person (such as those folks with the clipboards at your local mall), doing price comparisons, participating in taste tests or product trials, etc.

You may be asked to conduct exit interviews. This usually involves standing outside a business and asking questions of customers as they leave. You conduct these interviews with the knowledge of the manager—nothing mysterious here. Pay can be by the hour or by the completed survey.

Telephone Surveys

As a mystery shopper, you may perform mystery shops by telephone—that is, making a call to a catalog order desk or a customer service department, or calling a restaurant before your visit. Telephone surveys are different. A survey involves calling a client's customers or prospective customers and asking questions. This is not telemarketing, and telephone surveyers aren't selling anything.

Have you ever gotten a call from someone who wanted to know your opinion on something, or your experience with a company or product? That's a telephone survey.

Telephone surveys are often conducted with a client's customers, to get their opinions about the company. For example, after having a garage door opener installed, the company contacted me to make sure that the installer had been here on time, that he had done a good job, that the opener was working properly, that he had cleaned up after the job, etc. They wanted to be sure that the installer was doing a good job, and to take care of any problems if I wasn't satisfied.

You have been on the receiving end of telephone surveys, so you know how they work. When you perform a telephone survey, the questions you ask will be based on the client's information needs. You will be given a list of questions to ask, and the names and phone numbers of the people you are to call.

Telephone survey work may be available at call centers, or you may be able to get work that you can do from your own home.

Focus Groups

Focus groups are groups of people (anywhere from two or three people to more than 100) who answer questions or discuss issues relating to the client's business. Usually, group participants don't know who the client is. They are told only that someone wants their opinions about (for example) shopping for children's clothes. The group might include people who are current customers of the client, those who do business with their competitors, or a mixture. Focus groups are also used to gauge public opinion on political and social issues and for many other purposes.

When a large group is used, members of the focus group may each fill out a questionnaire and there may be little or no discussion. I have been a participant in focus groups for local radio stations where there are 100 or more participants. Each person is given a form with a number scale, and the market researchers play a few seconds from each of 600 songs. Participants give their opinions on the songs by circling the corresponding number on the form (e.g., don't like it, a favorite, etc.).

Many focus groups have six to twelve participants, and the members of the group talk about a issue. The discussion is usually recorded on video or audio tape, but the taping is done discreetly so it does not inhibit discussion.

Participants in focus groups are usually paid a fee ranging from $10 or $20 to $100 or more. Many people enjoy being a part of a focus group not only because of the money, but because they like having their opinions heard.

If you would like to be a participant in focus groups, contact some market research companies in your area and ask if you might qualify for any focus groups. Locate companies by looking in the local Yellow Pages under Market Research. Some companies will accept participants this way, but others take a position of "don't call us, we'll call you." Watch Help Wanted ads in your local newspaper. There are sometimes ads under General or Part Time headings for people to participate in market research studies and focus groups.

On the Internet there are sites which recruit participants in market research studies or to complete surveys, etc. Some pay in cash, while others award "points" which can be redeemed for merchandise. Before spending a lot of time filling out surveys, make sure you know exactly what you receive in return.

In-Store Demos

Demonstrators may show how a product works or they may give away samples or coupons. If you are outgoing and enjoy dealing with the public, you may find these to be a lot of fun.

In-store demos are often scheduled on weekends, so if you are available then it is a plus. Bi-lingual skills are useful, and sometimes required. Most jobs will have you in the store for four to six hours at a time, and you will be on your feet most or all of that time.

For more information, see the NARMS web site at http://www.narms.com/.

Organization and Record Keeping

As a mystery shopper, you may be responsible for completing many assignments during the course of a month. You may work for multiple mystery shopping companies and shop several clients for each.

Each evaluation may have a different time period in which it is to be done. Each client will have a different report format, and there may be unique requirements for each shop you do.

When you are a professional mystery shopper you have to juggle a variety of assignments and keep track of income and expenses for tax purposes. If you are not organized, it is easy to miss deadlines or forget to do things you are supposed to do. If you haven't kept track of your finances during the year, preparing your taxes can take longer than it should, and you may miss out on deductions you didn't record.

Fortunately, organizing your mystery shopping assignments doesn't have to be complicated. When you first start, and you are doing just a few assignments, mark them on the calendar and put the paperwork with other important papers (such as bills to be paid).

As the number of assignments available to you increases, you can set up a system that works for you. One easy way to do this is to get a file box and some file folders. Set up a folder for each assignment, and put all the paperwork for that assignment in the folder. The paperwork might include the assignment confirmation, guidelines, report forms, etc. Folders may be sorted by mystery shopping company, due date, or whatever works for you.

Keep track of due dates on a calendar reserved for that purpose. A large desktop calendar, with lots of room to write on it, works well.

Enter each shop in your computer as it is assigned to you. A spreadsheet program, such as Microsoft Excel, works well. Some shoppers use database or contact management software, such as Access or ACT!, or even Outlook. Include the name of the mystery shopping company and client, location, due date, fee, reimbursement, etc. You can use this file to monitor which shops you haven't completed, which you have, and to track payments as they are received.

Many shoppers find that *The Mystery Shopping Bible* is a useful tool. Mystery shopper Sherry Fox created it to manage her own mystery shopping business, and she has made it available to other shoppers.

The Mystery Shopping Bible is a sophisticated Excel spreadsheet, but it is easy to use. It allows you to track applications, assignments, expenses, payments and more. You can order your copy at Sherry Fox's web site, http://www.yourwebness.com/. At the web site, you can view screen shots from the spreadsheet, along with instructions and frequently asked questions.

Most companies suggest you keep copies of shop notes, reports and receipts for 60 to 90 days. That way, if there are any questions about the report or a receipt is lost in the mail, you can easily locate the information and resolve the problem.

Make a log of your auto mileage so you can claim any allowable mileage deductions on your tax return. A small notebook you keep in your car works well. Note the date, the purpose of your trip and the miles for each trip.

Other expenses can be recorded in a notebook or on your computer. Carry envelopes or file folders in your car, and file receipts and other shop documents immediately after you complete the shop.

Keeping to a routine may help you to stay on schedule. For example, set times when you will check job boards and forums, and seek new shopping opportunities. You might also want to schedule regular times to apply to additional companies, especially when you are starting out.

Plan when you will complete your shops, and remember to allow time to prepare. Schedule time as soon as possible after your shops to input reports.

If you can, check e-mail and voice mail at least twice a day. Respond promptly to any messages from schedulers and editors.

Make organizing and record keeping a regular part of your day. Get in the habit of recording expenses and filing your paperwork as the last step of each report.

Your organization system doesn't have to be complicated. It just has to work for you. You may want to experiment with different methods until you hit on the one you like best.

Technology and Mystery Shopping

Technology has made an impact on many industries, and mystery shopping is no exception. When I began mystery shopping in 1995, the Internet was not a factor in mystery shopping. I received assignments via postal mail and telephone, and submitted handwritten reports via mail and fax.

Times certainly have changed! These days, most companies work with shoppers almost exclusively through e-mail and the web (with some telephone contact). Sophisticated online systems have been developed to schedule shops, receive reports and generate data for clients. Even payment may be handled online, as more companies switch from paper checks to PayPal accounts.

Shoppers have more technology available to assist on shops. Digital cameras, digital recorders, cell phones, personal digital assistants (PDAs), laptop computers and other tools have delivered mystery shopping into the 21st century.

Online Mystery Shopping Systems

Most companies are using the Internet in some way to schedule shops and receive shop reports. Companies that do not have a dedicated online system may contact shoppers via e-mail to make assignments. Report forms may be Word or Excel documents that the shopper completes and e-mails back to the company.

Many companies use integrated systems designed specifically for mystery shopping. Some use proprietary systems they have developed in-house, and others use systems developed by outside vendors.

Two of the largest and best-known mystery shopping systems are SASSIE (which stands for Scheduling and Shopper Survey Internet Engine) and Prophet.

As a shopper, it will not matter to you what system a mystery shopping company uses; however, there are a few things you should know about them.

Prophet

The Prophet system was created by Archon Development. Prophet is used by more than 50 mystery shopping companies, who each customize the system to meet their reporting needs.

Although the mystery shopping companies that use Prophet do not share a common shopper database, shoppers may submit an application at the Archon Development web site that will be shared with any

Prophet users who wish to access it. To submit your application, go to http://apply.archondev.com/. After submitting your application, you may be contacted by mystery shopping companies to notify you that you have been added to their databases.

For more information about the Prophet system, go to http://www.archondev.com/.

SASSIE

Surf Merchants' SASSIE system is used by more than 50 mystery shopping companies around the world. Although these companies all use SASSIE, each company has their own SASSIE system and shopper information is not shared across systems.

Because each company activates the features they need to conduct their shops, there are differences in how each SASSIE system works when it comes to scheduling and reporting.

Most SASSIE sites have an online job board where you can search for shops within a specified number of miles of a zip code. You can use this to find local shops, or to locate assignments when you travel.

When submitting reports on SASSIE, save your work frequently to avoid losing any data. Simply click the "Submit" button whenever you want to save your work in progress.

For more information about the SASSIE system, go to http://www.sassieshop.com/.

Working with Online Systems

No matter what system a mystery shopping company uses, there are some things you should know about working with them.

Keep your profile updated. If your e-mail address changes, update it so you don't miss shop posting e-mails. When you obtain a certification, update your profiles with the certification number.

You will need to update your profile for each company to which you have applied. Remember that even the companies that use SASSIE or Prophet don't share shopper data with each other.

Make your profile as complete as possible. Companies sometimes add new fields when they get clients with specific requirements (e.g., digital camera, pet owner, specific make of car, etc.). Log in to your profile at each company from time and time and make sure all information is current.

Some, but not all, reporting systems have spell check available. If the report you are completing does not have spell check, you can use a browser-based spell check program such as ieSpell (available free at http://www.iespell.com/). Still proofread carefully.

If you are on AOL and have a problem with any system, minimize the AOL browser and go to the site using Internet Explorer.

Most systems have a Help feature. Click on it if you have a problem or aren't sure how to do something.

Your Computer

The type of computer and operating system you use may not matter, as long as you are able to access the Internet to get assignments and submit reports. If your operating system or Internet browser is out of date, you may have problems and need to get a newer version.

Your computer is an important mystery shopping tool. Keep it in good working order for the sake of your business. Install good virus checking software, and keep it updated. A virus can damage your system, as well as spreading itself to others through your computer.

Back up your computer often so that you don't lose data in the event of a system failure. I have an external hard drive that I use to back up every file on my computer at least weekly. Don't wait until you lose data. Put a back up system in place. And, keep at least one copy of your back up offsite. If a fire or other disaster were to destroy your office, you wouldn't want to lose your back up along with your computer.

Buying and Using Equipment

You may use equipment such as a digital camera, digital recorder, video recorder, laptop computer, cell phone or PDA during a shop. In some cases it will be a requirement, and other times you may choose to use the equipment to make it easier to capture the information you need.

The trend in mystery shopping is for clients to want more verification of shops. That means that there will be more demand, not less, for digital photos, videos, digital recordings of visits and telephone calls and other documentation. These media show and tell exactly what happened, with no reliance on one person's (the shopper's) word against another's (the employee's).

Companies doing video mystery shops will provide the equipment to you. However, if you find yourself doing many video shops, it might be worthwhile to invest in equipment of your own. Discuss this with the video mystery shopping company. They can assist you in obtaining the equipment and tell you what fee increase, if any, they offer for shoppers who provide their own video equipment.

The more equipment you own, the more shops for which you are eligible. That doesn't mean that you should go out and immediately buy a bunch of stuff. However, if you see a number of shop opportunities requiring equipment you don't have, that might be the time to think about investing in things that will help you to grow your business.

In some cases, the mystery shopping company will provide the equipment to you if you don't have it. However, your fee is usually higher if they don't have to ship things back and forth. The money you invest in equipment may be recovered quickly.

The equipment doesn't have to be expensive. You don't need a top of the line digital voice recorder. There are recorders in the $40 - $100 range that will do everything you need. You might also want to invest in a separate microphone for better recording quality. That will cost $20 - $30. A digital recorder for your phone line can cost $40 - $100. This device plugs into your phone line and records audio directly to your computer.

You may already own a digital camera that will work for mystery shops. The main issue is resolution (the picture quality). Know your camera's resolution and make sure it can produce photos of the required quality. Camera phones may work for some digital photo shops, but most do not have the resolution required for shops.

Laptops and PDAs are not often required at this time, but many shoppers find them useful. At some time in the future, they may become requirements.

Tips for Using Equipment

Practice using the equipment before you use it on a mystery shop. Be familiar with how it works, and how to operate it without drawing attention to yourself.

Turn off your cell phone before doing a shop. If you are going to use the cell phone during the shop, turn off the ringer so it does not disrupt the shop.

Check the batteries. Make sure your batteries are fully charged before starting the shop.

Have enough memory or storage available. You don't want to run out of memory before you have recorded the entire shop, or taken all of your photos.

If you are recording to an audio or video tape, make sure it is properly inserted and fully rewound.

When using a digital recorder, position it for maximum sound quality. If it is inside a purse the sound may be muffled and there may be rustling and other sounds interfering with recording. In a shirt pocket, it may be too close to your mouth. A side pocket or cell phone pocket can be a good location. Women can put the recorder or microphone in a bra.

Check all of your settings. For example, your digital camera must be set to the right resolution, and the flash should be off if you are taking photos discreetly.

Secure any buttons that could be accidentally pressed during the shop. You may place tape over them, or there may be a hold button that will prevent settings from being changed.

Preparing for the Shop

Whether you are a brand new or experienced mystery shopper, proper preparation is a critical part of completing your assignments correctly. Even if you have done a particular shop many times, always read the guidelines and report form before doing the shop. Clients make changes from time to time.

In fact, you should review your shop guidelines as soon as you receive them. Use a highlighter to identify key issues of the shop. If you have questions, this is the time to ask them. Don't wait until the day the shop is due. Most companies prefer that you contact them by e-mail, and the shop guidelines will probably tell you the best way to contact them. Give your scheduler time to respond.

You may discover that you are unable to meet the requirements of a shop. If you have to cancel an assignment, do it immediately. And, there should be a good reason. One male shopper told of having to cancel an assignment because he didn't think he could convince the employees that he was pregnant, a requirement of the shop. Because he immediately read the instructions, discovered he couldn't do the shop as required, and notified his scheduler, the shop could be reassigned right away.

If you are asked to confirm the shop, do so immediately. You can also take that opportunity to ask any questions you have about the shop.

If this is the first time you've shopped for this company, or the first time you've shopped this client, the mystery shopping company may want you to call to review the shop requirements over the phone. It gives them a chance to remind you of the most important aspects of the shop and make sure you understand what you are to do.

There may be things you have to do before going to the location, such as making a reservation or an appointment, or completing a telephone shop. Allow time to do these tasks before making the visit.

Don't assume that because you have been mystery shopping for a while, or because you have mystery shopped for the same company or client before, that you know what to do. Always read and follow the guidelines. Requirements vary from one client to the next, and even from one shop to the next for the same client.

Don't take the form with you to do the mystery shop. Instead, make a "tip sheet" you can refer to during the shop to remember all the things you are to do. For example, it might be helpful to have reminders of which departments you are supposed to visit, the things you need to time and the employees for which you need to get names.

The type of tip sheet you use will depend on the nature of the shop. It is critical that you not draw attention to yourself, so don't do anything that would make you stand out or make employees notice you.

You may want to make a few notes you can discreetly refer to during the shop. These notes might be on an index card tucked in a pocket or purse, buried in your shopping list, or on a sticky note tucked in your check register.

If you use a personal digital assistant (PDA), you may make some notes using the memo function, or perhaps even download the entire form to the PDA.

If you are doing a restaurant shop by yourself, you might take a crossword puzzle book with you. Hidden in the puzzle can be reminders such as, "manager," "server," and "hostess," to remind you of the names you need for the report.

Whether you are shopping by yourself or with a companion, you might have a day planner, travel planning materials, or classified ads. Make your tip notes discreetly in the materials, and you can refer to them during the shop while making it appear you are working on a project, planning a trip or looking for an apartment.

Many times, your tip sheet will also serve as a place where you can make notes during a shop. Of course, you must always take care not to be observed making notes about the shop.

There are times when it might not be appropriate to take a hard copy tip sheet in with you. However, you might be able to record a voice mail message for yourself with reminders of what you are to do on the shop. During the shop, use your cell phone to check your voice mail. Listen to the message you left for yourself, and you will be reminded of what you need to do on the shop.

Taking a Companion

If you are allowed or required to take someone with you on the shop, make sure they know what they are expected to do. Is there something they should or shouldn't ask? Will they help you with the shop by reading name tags or timing something? Or is their job to not get in the way while you do the shop? Go over their responsibilities carefully so that there are no mistakes and you get a valid shop.

Although it is your responsibility to get all of the required information, your companion may be able to help you obtain and remember some data. Let them know exactly what they need to do, and get the information from them immediately after the shop, before they forget.

It is critical that your companion understands the need for confidentiality, before, during and after the shop. Remind him that he is not to talk about mystery shopping during the shop, or do anything to give away the fact that you are the mystery shopper. And, he should not tell anyone that you are going to do a mystery shop, or that you have done one. This includes telling the people at the office about the great "free" dinner he had last night!

Preparation

The preparation you receive will vary from one company (and one client) to the next. You will always receive written guidelines on doing the shop. Some companies provide detailed manuals with all of their policies and procedures and everything you need to know about shopping for them.

Companies may want to conduct a telephone session with you, especially the first time you do a shop for them. It gives you the chance to ask any questions, and they can feel confident that you understand what is required of you.

In some circumstances you will receive face-to-face instruction. This might involve meeting with someone at an office, classroom training with other shoppers, or field training where you go into a business and conduct an actual shop or a test shop.

Whatever form your instruction takes, make sure you understand what you are supposed to do. If you have questions at any point in the process, ask for clarification. They want you to ask questions about anything you are not sure of.

Scenarios

In some cases, you will have to present a specific buying situation, or you will be pretending to be someone or something you are not. This is not dishonest–you are not doing it to deceive anyone, only to do the evaluation. It is simply a form of acting, and you will probably enjoy those occasions when you get to pretend.

If you are asked to use a scenario, the mystery shopping company will include information about the scenario in your guidelines. For example, they may offer suggestions regarding what you should say about why you are at that business. Why are you looking for an apartment? What kind of bank account are you interested in? Are you buying a cell phone for the first time, or are you thinking about changing carriers?

In addition to the information provided in the guidelines, consider how you will answer any questions you are asked. One shopper said she was shopping a bridal store and, because she is not married, she hadn't thought of answers to the questions they asked, such as the name of her fiancé, the wedding date, where they were going on their honeymoon, how many attendants she would have and what color they were wearing, etc.

When possible, you should keep your scenario as close to your reality as possible. In the bridal situation, if you are married you may be able to use the details of your own wedding to answer any questions. (You should also remove your wedding ring before doing the shop!)

Of course, you may not anticipate every question that could come up during a shop. If you are asked something that stumps you, there are several things you can do. You might act as though you didn't hear the question and ask them to repeat it, pretend you have forgotten or have to think about the answer, say you are unsure, or say that you would prefer not to give out too much personal information. The appropriate response depends on the situation. It would probably not be a good idea to act as though you have forgotten the name of your fiancé or say that you are unsure! However, it might be appropriate in a bank shop to say you are not sure how many checks you write each month, or that you would prefer not to give your name and address until you are ready to open an account.

Objections

In some shops you will have to leave without making a purchase, signing a contract or opening an account. In that case, you may raise an objection such as, "I need to talk to my spouse about this," or "There are a few other places I want to look before making a decision."

You may also be asked to raise a sales objection in order to test the employee's sales skills. The purpose of these objections is to give the employee an opening to sell to you.

Appropriate objections for a cell phone shop might include the cost of the phone or its features, not enough weekend minutes in the plan being presented, or the length of the contract. The sales person should have alternatives for each of these.

Apartment shops may require objections. Saying you don't like the neighborhood, or it is too far from your office doesn't give the rental agent an opportunity to sell to you. After all, they can't pick up the apartment community and move it somewhere more convenient for you! Good objections might include saying that you don't think your furniture will fit, you need more storage space, or you don't like the color of walls or carpets.

If the guidelines you receive don't suggest objections, and you aren't sure what objections might be appropriate, ask your scheduler for suggestions.

Doing a
Mystery Shop

Make sure you are thoroughly prepared before going to the location. Be certain to do the shop during the time frame required. If the shop is to be done between the 1st and the 10th of the month, do it then. If it is supposed to be done during certain hours of the day (e.g., dinner, between 5:30 and 7:30 p.m.) be sure to go at that time. And make sure you go to the right location. Double check the business name and the address.

What to Look For

The report form and guidelines tell you what to look for when doing the shop. You may be told to go to a certain department and ask questions about the merchandise, or check items to see if they are in stock.

You will usually go into the rest room to see if it is clean and well-stocked. In a restaurant, you may time how long before your order is taken, or until you got your food. You will check for safety hazards, such as puddles of water on the floor or merchandise stacked in the aisles.

How many cashiers were available? How many people were in line ahead of you? Is the facility clean? Did the salesperson offer you the extended warranty? You will get the names or descriptions of the employees you dealt with.

Each of the questions on the report form is there because the client needs to know about that aspect of his business. Make sure you get the information to answer each question accurately and completely. But don't stop there. If you notice something that isn't asked about on the form, whether it's good or bad, make a note of it. Remember to keep all comments objective. This is not about your personal taste and opinions.

One of the myths about mystery shopping is that the shopper is looking for what is wrong. Some think that if they haven't found a lot of "bad stuff" they haven't done their jobs as mystery shoppers. In fact, your job is to give an objective picture of your experience at the business.

Unless instructed otherwise, you shouldn't try to trick the employees being evaluated, or make it hard for them to do what they are supposed to do. Nor should you make it too easy by leading them to do the right thing. Think of yourself as a camera, recording what is happening. Do your best not to influence the outcome of a shop, either positively or negatively, with your behavior.

If the experience was great, that's good news. Most of the questions you are asked in your report call for objective answers. You are not writing a review, you are describing what happened—so tell it like it is, with the good, the bad, and the ugly!

When You Arrive

The shop begins before you've gotten out of your car. The report may include questions about the condition of the parking lot and building exterior, for example. If you can't be observed by employees, you may note the answers on your form before you get out of the car.

It's also a good idea to make a quick review of the form just before you go in. Read the items you highlighted to remind yourself what information you need to get. Check to see that you have your tip sheet tucked away in your pocket or purse. Make sure your watch is ready to time anything you need to time, and make a note of what time you are entering the business.

Getting Names

Most shops require that you get the names of the employees you observed. That can be easy if they are wearing name tags. Of course, you should be subtle about reading name tags. Don't stare or make a big deal about it. One shopper leaves her sunglasses on for the first few minutes, so employees can't tell where she is looking. Once she gets the names, she removes her sunglasses.

If an employee is not wearing a name tag, you may be able to get his or her name in another way. The receipt often gives the name of the cashier. You may hear the employee addressed by name by a customer or another employee. Be creative and you can often come up with a way to ask. For example, ask your server his name so you can ask for him next time you're in.

When you can't get a name, be sure to get a good description. Some reports will ask for description even if you have the name. Gender, race, height, weight, hair color and style, and distinguishing characteristics such as glasses or a beard may all be used to identify someone. Don't describe them using unflattering or insensitive descriptions, such as fat, foreign, etc.

Getting the Details

As you can tell, there is a lot to include in your reports. You probably won't be able to recall it all without making some notes as you do the shop (especially when you are new at this). Be discreet about making notes while you are doing the shop. Employees know that mystery shoppers are used, and if they know they are being shopped you won't get an accurate picture.

You will almost always have to check the rest room. That is a good place to make notes about what you have observed to that point, and review your tip sheet to remind yourself what else you need to do.

When doing a retail shop, you may be able to carry a shopping list and make notes there.

During a shop, you might be able to use the pay phone or your mobile phone to leave a voice mail message with names or other observations you need to have for your report. Of course, you should only do this if you are certain you won't be overheard by employees.

If you can't make notes during the shop, record as much information as possible as soon as you leave. You might go to your car (out of sight of the employees) and write information on the report form, or use a digital or micro-cassette recorder to record the information you need for the report while it is still fresh in your mind.

Many shoppers like to use digital recorders as a way to record what happens during shops. Some recorder models include timers, so you can use the recording to verify the timings you need for the shop.

Digital cameras can be useful for taking quick snapshots of a scene you want to be able to describe in your report. Camera phones may work best, as they are less obvious and it is easier to conceal that you are taking a photo.

Several companies are now using hidden video cameras to record the entire shop. This is especially true when the client wants to see and hear what the employee did during a presentation, such as for home builders, apartment complexes, banks and car dealerships. However, video shopping is used for retail, restaurant and other shops as well. If you are asked to videotape the shop, the company will provide the equipment and teach you how to use it. The equipment is so small that a camera may be hidden in a button or a piece of jewelry. The best part about videotaping a shop is that you may not have to write a report!

Memory Tips

Having a good memory is useful when you are mystery shopping. There are many details to remember, such as names, times, what employees said to you, etc. The more details you can recall accurately, the more valuable your report will be.

There are many memory techniques that can help you retain names and other details. If you are having a conversation with an employee, you might try using the employee's name once or twice during the conversation. Only do this if it sounds natural.

Some people are good at constructing rhymes that help them remember names and details. Others use associations.

You might try setting what you are trying to remember to music and playing the tune in your head. When I was a little girl, my mother set the Girl Scout Pledge to music, and wrote a song to help my troop memorize the Girl Scout Laws. To this day, I can recall the pledge and all ten laws because I remember the songs.

Practice, practice, practice. The more you exercise your memory, the better it will become. The next time you are in a store, practice remembering the details you typically need to recall on a mystery shop. Try different memory techniques until you find the ones that work best for you.

Taking Someone with You

You may want to take your spouse, child or friend with you when you are mystery shopping. Make sure that it is allowed before taking anyone along on a shop.

When asked, "May mystery shoppers bring their children along on shops?" the answers given by mystery shopping companies ranged from, "Yes," to "Sometimes," to "Never!" You should never take *anyone* along with you if they will be a distraction or interfere with the shop in any way.

There may even be times when you are asked to take your children or someone else with you, because of a client requirement. However, if the shop instructions say you should go alone, or say not to bring children, follow those instructions. The instructions for restaurant shops often suggest or require that you have a companion. If you want to take your children, contact the mystery shopping company and make sure children are allowed before you do so.

In general, you may be able to take your children on a shop if it is a place you would normally take them (for example, to a fast food restaurant, but probably not fine dining). But never assume that your children are welcome to accompany you on a shop. Always ask the mystery shopping company.

Whenever someone accompanies you on a shop, it is your responsibility to see that they know what to do. Explain the important instructions to them before you go. For example, you might be asked not to order an appetizer until your server has had a chance to suggest one. If the first words out of your companion's mouth are, "Bring us an order of fried cheese," you haven't followed the shop instructions.

Your companion must also understand the need for secrecy. They must not do anything to give away the fact that you are mystery shopping.

Remember That You Are a "Mystery" Shopper

When you are doing a shop, you must not let anyone know that you are a mystery shopper. The whole idea is that you want to see how the typical customer is treated. If they know you are a mystery shopper, you will not have a typical experience.

Don't tell anyone who works for the store that you are mystery shopping, and don't talk about mystery shopping with any companions you have. If you have children with you, don't tell them you are doing a mystery shop if they are likely to share this information with anyone who happens to be around.

Don't carry your report form with you. Some companies will provide a tip sheet which you can fold up and carry to remind you of what you need to do on the shop. Be discreet when you take any notes. Many times, you can carry a shopping list and make your notes there.

Don't do anything to draw unnecessary attention to yourself. Unless the guidelines say otherwise, don't complain or ask to speak to a manager about anything.

You may feel very conspicuous, especially the first few times you go mystery shopping. It may seem to you that you have a large neon sign on your forehead, flashing MYSTERY SHOPPER. In fact, no one will know that you are a mystery shopper.

I've had to ask questions or do things that I was sure would alert all the employees that I was checking up on them. In reality, no one noticed or thought anything about it. The employees know that their location is mystery shopped; however, they often don't know exactly what the mystery shopper will do or ask. And, frankly, real shoppers will do odder things than we are asked to do!

If you are really concerned about it, construct a couple of possible scenarios ahead of time, and plan how you would deal with them. For example, what would you say if an employee asked if you are a mystery shopper? It's not going to happen, but if you're worried about it, plan a response.

One answer would be, "No, I'm not." The best way to handle it is probably to act like you've never heard of mystery shopping. You will end the questioning quickly by asking, "Mystery shopper? What's that?"

I did a number of shops where I was required to return something I had purchased only minutes before. I was certain that at worst, they would immediately know I was a mystery shopper, and at best, they would think it was odd. Therefore, I concocted all sorts of stories as to why I was returning items I'd just bought: I thought this purse would match the shoes I bought at another store, I picked up the wrong size, etc. *They never asked any questions, they just processed my return.* So, while you should try not to draw attention to yourself, don't be overly concerned about being identified as a mystery shopper.

Telephone Mystery Shopping

You may be asked to do some shops by telephone. For example, a hotel chain or airline might want to evaluate its reservations agents, an insurance company its claims staff, or a mail order company its phone order takers. Telephone shops are often a part of restaurant, bank and retail shops, too.

Just as in the in-person shops, you will have a list of questions to answer. You may be able to complete the report while you are on the phone, from memory or your notes after you hang up, or you may tape the call. Some companies are now asking you to record the shop as an MP3 file. They may give you a toll-free number to call and a code to enter to activate the recording equipment. You then make the mystery shop call and it is recorded in MP3 format and sent to the client.

When you are required to complete a written report of a telephone shop, questions may include:

How many rings before you received an answer?

Did you have to make more than one attempt before getting a ring?

Was the phone answered by a person or a recorded message?

Did the person who answered give their name? Name:_____

How long were you on hold?

Ask (assigned question). Was the associate able to answer your question?

Was the associate courteous? Did s/he sound like s/he was smiling?

Did the associate encourage you to come in?

Did s/he thank you for calling?

Digital Photo Shopping

Some shops require that you use a digital camera to take photos during the mystery shop. You may be asked to photograph people, products, buildings and signage or equipment. In some cases you will let the manager know that you will be taking photographs, and in other cases you must take the photographs without being noticed.

Digital photographs may accompany a written report, or they may be used in place of a written report. Although you can be a mystery shopper without owning a digital camera, having one makes you eligible for the shops that require digital photographs.

The guidelines will specify the file format and resolution you are to use for the photographs. Some files can be large, so it helps to have a high-speed Internet connection when uploading them.

Video Mystery Shopping

Have you ever imagined yourself going undercover, like one of those TV reporters with a hidden camera? That is very much what it is like when you do a video mystery shop.

During a video mystery shop you will do many of the same types of things you do in a regular mystery shop. You will ask questions of employees, engage them in conversations and record their responses. You may also be asked to record images of the sales floor and service areas.

An advantage of video over written reports is that the client can see exactly what happened, and not have to rely on the written impressions of the mystery shopper. The employee who was shopped can view the tape and see exactly how they come across to customers.

The video equipment is easily hidden. The camcorder and battery pack are usually worn on a belt or carried in a purse. The camera itself it so small that it can be hidden in a button or a piece of jewelry.

Shoppers hired to do video shopping often have experience in mystery shopping or using video equipment. If you are asked to do a video mystery shop, you will be taught how to use the equipment and conduct the shop.

You may be asked to do some sample or test shops to get used to using the equipment. According to the companies that do video shopping, the best way to learn is to do a shop then view the tape you made. You can immediately see your results that way. Test shops allow you to learn without the pressures of a real shop.

The mystery shopping company will provide the video equipment for you. You may pick it up from a local location or it will be shipped to you.

Video mystery shoppers often receive higher fees than mystery shoppers doing a standard written report. Fees start at about $30 and can go up to $150 or more.

For more information on shopping with digital and video cameras, see the section on Technology and Mystery Shopping.

Tips for
Apartment Shops

Mystery shops of apartment complexes are designed to test the rental consultant's sales skills. Often, the shops are targeted, meaning that you will be asked to make an appointment to visit with a specific rental agent. During the visit you will do the things that a person looking for apartment normally does. You'll talk about your needs, look at apartments and listen to the agent present the features and benefits of the apartment complex. If you have ever rented an apartment, you should have no problem conducting an apartment mystery shop.

Here are some tips to help make your apartment mystery shop go smoother.

Read the instructions for the shop carefully in order to understand exactly what is required and if there is a specific scenario you are to present.

Get comfortable with your scenario. You may be given a specific scenario by the mystery shopping company, or you may have some latitude to create a story of your own. The scenario you present will include things like the size of apartment you're looking for, the date you plan to move in, the number of persons who will live in the apartment, whether or not you have pets, a price range, any special needs or qualifications you have, and how you heard about the apartment complex. Prior to visiting the apartment complex, makes sure that they advertise in the place you plan to mention.

When you visit, you will have to present a valid form of identification such as a driver's license. This means you must give your real name, address and telephone number. You may also be asked the name of your employer. If you are currently employed, you may give the name of your actual employer. If not, make up an employer or mention some place you formerly worked. Don't tell them that you are a mystery shopper.

Prior to your visit you will have to contact the agent by phone and make an appointment. This is an important part of the shop. Because you're calling for a particular agent, it may take several phone calls before you reach the correct agent. It is a good idea to press *67 on your telephone to block caller identification so the apartment complex doesn't know that you called multiple times.

Plan to spend at least 30 minutes touring the apartment community. If the car you drive does not fit the demographic profile of the apartment community, you should park out of sight of the leasing office. Don't take any of your shopping paperwork in with you, and don't take notes during the mystery shop. Many shoppers find it useful to carry a digital recorder to record the shop and their observations.

During the shop, you may be asked to present an objection. The purpose of this is to test the rental agent's sales skills. Therefore, your objection should not be one that stops the conversation, but one that gives an opening to the rental agent to sell you on the apartment. An example of a poor objection would be that you want to look at several other places. That's fine at the end of the presentation when you want to get out without signing a lease; however, there is no good way for the rental agent to overcome this objection.

Examples of good objections would include: "There doesn't seem to be enough closet space," "I don't think my sofa will fit in the living room," or "I don't care for the color of the walls." The rental agent should attempt to overcome your objection to show you how the apartment can work for you. If the agent does not attempt to overcome your objection, make light of it yourself and move on. Don't let this objection to be a stopping point for the conversation or prevent the agent from closing you as a result of it.

Be interested in the apartment. Remember, you're not actually going to live there, you just have to act as though you are a potential renter. You might say things such as, "It would be great to have barbecues out here on the patio," or "I love having the washer and dryer right here in the apartment."

Apartment shops also address issues such as fair housing and safety. You need to be subtle about these questions. For example you might ask whether there are other families with children in the complex, or if there are problems with burglaries or vandalism in the area.

Once you have visited the apartment, the leasing agent should try to close you and get you to sign a lease. They may do this by asking questions such as, "Are you ready to fill out an application?" or "Would you like me to hold the apartment for you?" They may also say things to create a sense of urgency such as, "This is the last apartment I have available right now." This is when you use your objection that you are looking at several communities and you're not ready to make a decision at this time. Do not identify yourself as the mystery shopper or tell them that you are not really looking for apartment.

Many companies will also ask you to report any follow-up contacts made by the rental agent. If you receive a telephone call, e-mail or thank you note, you should report it to the mystery shopping company.

Tips for Bank Shops

There are many kinds of bank shops. Including:
    Drive-through where you conduct a transaction from your car in the drive-through lane.

    Lobby Teller where you make a transaction such as a deposit or withdrawal inside the bank.

    Platform where you ask about opening a new account.

    Mortgage or Loan where you inquire or apply for a loan.

Additionally, shops may be done over the telephone to a branch or call center, or online.
    Matched pair testing uses two shoppers presenting identical financial profiles, but varying by race or gender.

For some bank shops, a current customer of the bank is required or preferred. For others, it doesn't matter.

If you are a customer of the bank, it is easy to do a transaction such as a deposit or withdrawal. If you are not a customer, you may be able to buy or cash traveler's checks or complete another transaction that does not require an account.

Where you bank doesn't matter for shops where you inquire about applying for a loan or opening an account.

Be prepared. You may be presenting a financial profile that varies from your reality, perhaps that you have a large sum of money to invest. Know your scenario well.

Don't be too knowledgeable about the bank. Don't say, "I need to speak with a PBR," just say you want information about opening a new account.

If you are shopping far from home, have a reason for being in that bank. You are moving to the area, you recently got a job there, etc. "Just passing through" is not a good reason to be there asking about a new account!

Look for local businesses and neighborhoods you can refer to if they ask about your new house or new job.

Keep your story simple. Don't make it too complicated to remember.

Don't volunteer a lot of information. Let the employee lead the conversation, and simply respond to their questions.

You may be asked about your current bank accounts and investments, including how much money you keep in your accounts, how many checks you write, if you own your home, if you have consumer loans or credit cards, etc.

Depending on the scenario, you may give your actual information or a fictional profile. The shop guidelines should help you prepare the answers you will need to give. Some shops require that you present a specific scenario, and the guidelines will tell you what responses to give. If you have any questions, ask your scheduler.

Don't be defensive or difficult about answering these questions. They are asking in order to match you to the best products and services. If you are uncomfortable with some of the detailed questions, you may be able to defer them, saying you would prefer to provide that information after you have selected an account.

Employees may be expected to cross-sell and recommend additional products, or tell you about a promotion, such as a special interest rate on CDs. Listen for this–it's important.

Mystery shoppers must be observant, but don't "case the joint." Don't do anything that would cause employees to become suspicious or nervous.

Opening multiple accounts in the same day, or conducting transactions at multiple locations, can get you flagged as a security risk. Ask your scheduler how many shops you can do within a given period without being flagged.

If think you have been identified as the shopper or as a security risk, notify your scheduler. The scheduler will handle the situation with the bank. Don't tell the bank employees that you were shopping them.

Tips for
Restaurant Shops

The time of visit is important. You will be given a range of times, such as between 5:30 p.m. and 8:30 p.m. for a dinner shop. Don't do the shop outside of those hours.

You may be asked to get many timings during your shop. Fast food shops often require several timings to the second. Use a stopwatch with a lap timer to record multiple times. The stopwatch should be concealed in a pocket so you can time discreetly.

A digital recorder with a timer can be a good way to capture timings at full-service restaurants.

Restaurant shops often allow or require that you take someone with you. Your companion must understand any requirements regarding what is to be ordered. You may be prohibited from ordering alcohol, or you may be limited to one alcoholic beverage per person. There may be requirements regarding the types of food items you should order (e.g., one appetizer, two entrees, two beverages and one dessert), and you will be expected to order different items.

My husband and I often download the menu from the restaurant's web site and plan what we are going to order before we get to the restaurant. That way, we know that we have selected different items, we have planned how we will order from each category, and we can concentrate on doing the shop instead of studying the menu. Don't be over-prepared, though. Allow the server to suggest items.

Refer to the guidelines regarding how many people may accompany you. If the guidelines state two adults only, it means exactly that. Don't take more adults and don't take your children along.

If the shop includes a bar visit, pay attention to whether you are asked to visit the bar before or after dinner.

Bar visits may allow you to order one or two alcoholic beverages per person. Typically, you and your companion are not both required to drink, although it may be recommended or required that at least one of you order an alcoholic beverage.

Don't be a big spender and order the most expensive items on the menu. Be a typical diner. That goes for tipping, too. The guidelines usually allow for a tip in the range of 15 - 20%.

Don't make notes at the table, and NEVER bring out the report form in the restaurant.

The report must be objective. The food isn't "poor" because you don't like anchovies.

Writing Reports

Once you have done the shop visit, the next step is to complete the report. Don't be surprised if it takes longer than you expect to do your first few reports. Like most things, it will get easier with experience.

The time required to complete your report may range from a few minutes for a simple check-off form with a few comments, to hours for an extensive narrative. Although your fee is not usually expressed as an hourly rate, companies consider the relative ease or difficulty of completing the report, and the time that may be required, when setting fees.

Before writing your report, gather anything you need: forms to complete, log-in information if the forms are online, notes or recordings you made during the shop, the guidelines and/or sample reports, receipts and other documents, etc.

Most reports are completed online; however, some reports may be typed or handwritten and faxed or mailed, and others will be phoned in to the mystery shopping company. Some shops will not require a written report. Instead, you will submit an audio or video recording, or a digital photograph.

Do it Now!

The report should be written immediately after completing the shop, while your memories are strong. Most companies require that the report must be completed within 24 hours after the shop, but some are due even sooner.

Report Types

Most report forms have a series of yes or no questions. For example, the report may ask if the cashier said thank you, and you would select yes or no, depending on whether or not the cashier thanked you.

These questions typically include "N/A" (Not Applicable) as a possible answer. However, you should only choose N/A when the question truly does not apply. For example, if you are asked if the parking lot was properly lighted, and you do the shop during daylight hours. Never select N/A because you forgot the answer or didn't check something.

You may also see rating questions on reports. These types of questions ask you to supply a rating or ranking based on a numeric scale (e.g., rate the quality of the food on a scale from 1 to 10) or a scale such as poor, fair, good, very good, excellent.

When you are asked to give a rating, the client will typically define what the ratings mean. Some might say that if the standards are met that is a 10. Others might say that a 10 should only be given if the quality or service is truly extraordinary.

Most reports will also require that you provide some comments and/or a narrative. Comments are almost always required for any "no" answers on the report, and you may be asked to provide at least a few comments for each section of the report.

You may also be asked to provide a short narrative, describing what happened during the shop.

Although not the most common type of report, some reports are all narrative. This means that you will write a description of everything that happened from the beginning of the shop until the end, usually in chronological order. This type of report may require writing a page or two, or it may be many pages long for a complex shop. The guidelines you receive will explain what should be included in the report and any requirements regarding the length of the report.

The type of report used for an assignment will usually be described in the offer of an assignment. For example, the offer may say that the report is a check-off form with a brief comments section, or a two-page form with a three-paragraph narrative required. Sometimes, you can review the actual form before deciding if you will accept an assignment.

Timings

Reports will also ask for timings. At a minimum, you will be asked what time you arrived and usually what time you left. You may also be asked how long you were in line, how long it took to receive your food, how long you were in the store before you were greeted, etc.

Timings may be expressed as a time of day (e.g., 4:37 p.m.) or as an elapsed time (e.g., 2:47 for two minutes and 47 seconds). Read the form carefully to determine which format you should enter. Both may be used within the same report. For example, you might be asked what time you ordered your entree (time of day), how many minutes later it was served (elapsed time) and how long after that the server returned to perform the satisfaction check (elapsed time).

Some timings will be to the minute, and others will be to the second. Enter the times as specifically and accurately as possible.

Completing the Report Form

The notes or other documentation you obtained during the shop will provide the answers you need for the report. Refer to the guidelines if you are not sure how some questions should be interpreted and answered.

Your answers must be honest and fair. Remember that it is your job to report what happened as it happened. Don't try to make employees look bad or make excuses for poor performance. Simply report what they did.

Answer every question on the form. Each question is there for a reason.

Because most reports are now completed using a computer, it is unlikely that you will be asked to handwrite your report. However, if anything is handwritten, your writing must be neat and legible.

Never falsify any information on a report. The information you provide is important to the client. It may even be used to determine raises and bonuses for employees. And, clients are increasingly seeking ways to verify mystery shopping reports, so inaccuracies will be discovered.

Before submitting your report, check it over to make sure it is complete and correct. Look for unanswered questions, data entry errors, misspelled words, missing or inconsistent comments, or anything else that will cause the mystery shopping company to call you. If your report is incomplete, your fee may be reduced or withheld. A pattern of poor reports means you won't receive future assignments.

Working Online

Completing reports online is similar to filling out other online forms. If you have ever completed a survey or ordered merchandise online, you know how to fill out an online form. Online report forms contain radio buttons (where you click to choose an answer), drop-down boxes (where you select the best answer from a group of choices) and fill-in boxes (where you key in a text answer).

Some systems will automatically log you out after a certain amount of time, or if you haven't entered any data for a certain amount of time. If you haven't saved your data, it could be lost.

Some systems will allow you to save your report multiple times. When you save an incomplete report, the system will notify you that your report is not finished and allow you to go back to the form and continue entering data. Some systems will save each section of the report as you complete it, so if there is any interruption you can simply log in again and continue where you left off.

Many reports require a minimum number of characters in each comment section. For example, you might be asked to provide at least 100 characters of comment about your interaction with the sales person. The system will not accept your report unless you have at least 100 characters in that section. Conversely, some reports have a maximum number of characters.

It is always a good idea to print or save a copy of your report. Although rare, system "glitches" can happen, and your report may be lost. If you have a saved copy, you can easily resubmit the report and not have to start over from the beginning.

After Submitting the Report

In addition to submitting the report, you may need to send a copy of a receipt, business card or other documentation. A few companies may ask you to send an invoice.

When you are asked to submit documents such as receipts, the preferred method is usually to scan and e-mail the receipt. The second choice is to fax it. If you don't have access to a scanner or fax machine, most companies will allow you to submit receipts by postal mail.

When faxing anything to companies, make sure you are faxing to the correct company. Many mystery shopping companies have told me that they have received receipts and reports intended for other companies.

Save the notes and documentation from your shop in case there are any questions about your report. Most companies suggest saving all shop documents for at least 60 to 90 days after you complete the assignment. Set up a filing system so that you can quickly and easily retrieve the paperwork from a shop if it is needed.

After you submit your report it will be reviewed by an editor, then forwarded to the client. Some companies will provide feedback about your report. This usually takes the form of a rating or grade. For example, a company might use a scale of one to ten, with ten being the best.

Of course, your goal is to get perfect scores on your reports, but don't be overly concerned if your rating is an eight or nine on a ten-point scale. Usually, a ten means that you submitted a report that the editor didn't have to fix: all of the required comments were there, all questions were answered, there were no spelling or grammar errors, etc. However, some editors might only give a nine for a report like that, and reserve tens for reports that go above and beyond the requirements.

If your report is given a rating, you may get an e-mail from the editor with the rating and any comments. Don't expect a detailed analysis of your report. The editors don't have time for that. They might just say, "Great report!" Or, you might see a comment such as, "Please watch your spelling," or "This report could have used more detail."

Writing Employee Descriptions

You may be asked to provide a description of the employees with whom you interacted. The description is especially important when you are unable to obtain the employees' names, but you may be asked to provide a description in addition to names.

The mystery shopping company will tell you what characteristics you should include in your description. For example, most do not ask for race, but some will. Common characteristics are gender, age range, height, hair color and length or style, and other distinguishing features. (We will get back to that one.)

In some cases, you will select descriptors from drop-down menus on the online report form. For example, the form might ask for "Hair color," and the menu choices could include: blonde, black, brown, red, no hair, other. The choice of "other" would require you to enter the color, such as, "purple."

Other report forms may have blanks for you to fill in each descriptor. For example, there will be boxes for you to enter the age range, height, hair color and other distinguishing features of the employee.

Or, you may be asked to enter the descriptions as part of your comments. In this case, the company will explain which characteristics to include. Follow their guidelines and the tips below.

Age: You won't know the employee's exact age, so use a range such as 20's.

Height: If you are standing next to the employee, estimate based on your own height. It can be difficult to determine height when you are seated and the employee is standing, or when the employee is on a raised surface, such as a platform, but make your best estimate. Keep heights relative to each other. If you believe the first employee is 5'5" and the next is a little taller, estimate that he is 5'6".

Hair color, length and style: Be as specific as possible. For example, "Shoulder-length black hair," is better than "Medium-length dark hair."

Other distinguishing features: This is where it gets interesting. What are "distinguishing features"? They may include eyeglasses, facial hair (on men only!), tattoos, body piercings, or even distinctive clothing or jewelry. Don't mention anything that might be hurtful or offensive, such as physical disabilities (e.g., limp, speech impediment) or large size (e.g., fat, heavy, obese). Stay away from politically incorrect observations, such as referring to someone as "foreign." And never identify a female employee as "pregnant" unless you are absolutely certain.

Reports are typically sent to the manager of the location you shopped. The manager may share reports with the employees who were shopped, or even post them on a bulletin board for everyone to read. How would you like being described as the "fat woman with the foreign accent who limped"?

One mystery shopper said that the guideline she uses when deciding whether to include something in a description was if the employee has control over it. For example, the employee did not choose to walk with a limp, but did choose to grow a beard and get a tattoo. This is generally a good guideline to follow.

Writing Comments and Narratives

Most reports will require at least a few comments. Typically, you will be asked to provide a comment for each question you answer with a "no." The guidelines may also specify that you are to provide a minimum number of comments, words or characters for each section of the report.

Some companies will provide a sample report to illustrate how the report should be completed, the number of comments to include and the level of detail to include in the comments. If you receive a sample, follow the format as closely as possible but don't copy the words exactly. While some clients love having lots of comments, others want very few. The sample will give you an idea of what they expect.

All of the information you provide should be as objective as possible. You are reporting what happened, not writing a review. Don't say the food was bad, say why. Was it cooked improperly? Cold? Stale? Not what you ordered? Be specific. Don't say that the food was poorly prepared because you don't happen to like the flavor.

Don't say the wait was "too long," say you waited 10 minutes before you reached the cashier. Saying the manager was helpful isn't very clear. Saying that you saw him carry trays for a mother dining with three small children tells exactly what happened.

Use names or descriptions of employees. The client wants to know who is doing a great job, and who is doing a not-so-great job. Telling him is *your* job.

Answer each question on the form. Add comments to back up both positive and negative ratings. Make sure that your answers are consistent with your comments. If you answer a question that, yes, the salesperson served you promptly, but in your comments say that you had to wait five minutes while he finished a personal call, that doesn't add up!

Remember that you're giving an objective picture of what you saw, and you're not trying to find things wrong. Don't look for excuses to give a poor rating. Be honest and fair. One tissue on the rest room floor doesn't mean that the rest room wasn't clean. (C'mon, you know right away when a rest room isn't clean, don't you?) Of course, if the guidelines for the shop say that any flaw is reason for a "no" answer, follow the guidelines.

If you are not sure how to answer a question, e-mail or call the mystery shopping company and ask. Let's say the evaluation form asks if the salesperson offered you the Premium Gold Maintenance Plan. Your salesperson told you a service contract is available, but didn't specifically mention the Premium Gold Maintenance Plan by name. Do they get a yes or a no? That depends on the company's service standard. When in doubt, contact the mystery shopping company and ask. If you are unable to contact the mystery shopping company before the report is due, give your best answer and explain in the comments exactly what happened.

Keep your comments objective, and focused on what you observed. Don't tell them what they should do, tell them what you saw. For example, don't say that the floor "needed to be mopped." Say that the floor was dirty, especially the baseboards and in the corners, or that there was a puddle of standing water 12" wide. Instead of "trash needed to be emptied" say that the trash can was overflowing onto the floor.

If you are required to do a narrative report, you will be told what you must include, and how long the report should be at minimum or maximum. Follow the guidelines as closely as possible.

Some companies will appreciate it if you go beyond the questions you are required to answer in a form or narrative report, and mention anything notable. Did you see an employee go out of his way to help a customer? Was the sneeze guard missing from the salad bar? Was a loose tile causing a safety hazard? Provide any observations that you might want to know about if you owned that business.

Your reports must be organized and easy to follow. Put comments in the correct locations. You may be asked to number your comments to correspond to the questions on the form. Whatever the instructions, make sure you follow them.

Sample Comments

Here are some examples of comments that should not be in a report, and how those same observations could be better expressed.

I had to wait in line a really long time.
This is not specific. What is a "really long time" to you might not be to someone else. It doesn't tell what your experience was. A better way to say this would be:
There were five customers in line ahead of me. I waited in line 13 minutes before reaching the cashier.
Other details it might be appropriate to add include:
Four of the nine checkout lanes were open. After I had been in line for nine minutes, the Manager manned a register and opened a fifth lane.

Lynda was polite and helpful.
That's nice, but what did Lynda do to cause you to characterize her as polite and helpful? Describe actions and behaviors.
Lynda greeted me 12 seconds after I entered, saying, "Hi! Can I help you find something?" She smiled and made eye contact. When I told her I was just looking, she said to ask if I needed anything.

Steve was very rude. He needs to learn to treat customers better.

"Very rude" doesn't tell us what Steve did. Did he ignore you, say something inappropriate, tell you to take your business elsewhere . . . what did he do? The second sentence is an unnecessary opinion.

No one greeted me when I entered. Steve and Jan were having a conversation behind the counter. I approached and asked where I could find toothpaste. Steve sighed and said, "Aisle five," then went back to his conversation.

The rest room was disgusting.

I'm sure you have the idea by now. This doesn't tell us anything about what was wrong with the rest room.

The maintenance schedule in the women's rest room was last initialed at 3:00 p.m., three hours before my visit. The trash can was full, and trash was spilling onto the floor. One of the three toilets was not working, and had overflowed.

The dining room was elegantly decorated. The walls were beige and there were brass railings and fixtures throughout. They know what the dining room looks like. This comment could be left out completely. You might want to comment on the cleanliness instead:

The carpets, walls and ceiling tiles were spotless. The brass railings and fixtures were bright and shiny.

Service was slow. I think someone may have called in sick.
The first sentence is vague. The second is speculation. These comments don't belong in your report. Only comment on facts that you know to be true. If you were told that someone called in sick, you might include it as follows:

Our entrees were served 19 minutes after we ordered. Thirteen minutes after we ordered, Carla came to our table to apologize for the delay. She said that the assistant chef had called in sick, but the kitchen staff would have our food out in a few minutes.

Sample Narrative Report

The sample report on the next two pages is provided to give you an idea of what a narrative might look like and what kind of information may be included.

This report is only an example. If you are required to write a narrative report be sure to follow the guidelines you are given regarding length, level of detail, specific issues to address, etc.

Sample Narrative Report

Restaurant: Mama's Hacienda
Location: My Town, USA

Day: Thursday   Date: Sept. 27
Time of visit: 6:15 p.m. - 7:10 p.m.

My guest and I entered the restaurant and were immediately approached by a hostess (Monica). She greeted us, asked our seating preference, and seated us at a booth in the non-smoking section, as requested.

Jason greeted us 30 seconds after we were seated and brought water, chips and salsa to the table. He also offered green sauce.

Our waiter, Miguel, arrived within two minutes and asked for our drink order. We ordered margaritas, and he asked if we preferred our drinks frozen or on the rocks. Miguel suggested the Amazin' Onion appetizer, and we ordered one.

The drinks (frozen) were served in frosted mugs, with salt around the rims and a lime wedge garnish. They were thick enough that the straws stood up in the mugs, but we were able to drink them through the straws. The margaritas were properly tart, but we could not taste any tequila in them.

The Amazin' Onion was presented on a platter with a dipping sauce in the center. The batter on the onion was soggy, not crisp, but the flavor was good.

I ordered the Cheeseburger Platter. The burger was served open-faced, with lettuce, tomato and onion.

A pickle and french fries filled the rest of the platter. The burger was prepared as ordered, and was cooked as specified. The burger and french fries were hot, and the garnish and pickle were cold and crisp. The bun was fresh, the beef of high quality, and the fries crisp and golden.

My companion ordered the Gringo Special, which included a taco, a burrito and an enchilada, with sides of rice and beans. The appearance of the plate was excellent, with the food presented in an appetizing and colorful way. All food was served hot, except the lettuce, onion and tomato garnishes which were cold and crisp. The food was all excellent, except the refried beans, which were watery.

Our used plates were cleared promptly by Miguel and Jason during the meal. Additional drinks were offered, and water glasses were refilled often. All food portions were generous. We asked for extra napkins and were given several.

Miguel returned to ask for our dessert order. He presented the dessert tray and knowledgeably answered our questions. We selected the chocolate cake and the raspberry cheesecake. Both were served in generous portions and had excellent flavor.

Miguel brought the check as we finished our dessert. I paid by credit card, and he returned promptly with my receipt. As we left, both Miguel and Monica thanked me by name.

My guest and I agreed that we had a pleasurable dining experience, and we would return to Mama's Hacienda.

Tips for Writing Comments and Narratives

Stick to the facts. Don't offer your opinions unless they are specifically requested. Watch out for "I" language, such as, "I think," "I feel," or "I believe." These are opinions.

Think of yourself as a fly on the wall. Report what you observed.

Be specific. Avoid vague words such as very, really, so, lots, a lot, kind of, sort of, about, approximately, etc.

Avoid extreme language, such as always and never, and extreme negatives such as horrible, gross, or disgusting.

Don't be dramatic. Stick to reporting the facts and stay away from comments along the lines of, "I have never received such poor service in my life."

Tell what you found, not what they should do about it. "There was a 12" puddle of water in the entryway," is better than, "The floor needed to be mopped."

"Sandwich" negative comments with positive ones. You are required to give comments for the questions to which you answered "no." However, try to avoid having all negative comments. They did *something* right, didn't they? Mention it.

Never cut-and-paste comments from one report to another. Each experience is unique, and your report should reflect that unique experience.

Don't make comparisons to other locations, other visits or other businesses. Comment only on the shop visit.

Make sure your comments are consistent with each other and with the answers to report questions. If you answer yes to the question, "Were all employees wearing name tags?," but in your comments say that you don't know the name of the employee who assisted you because he wasn't wearing a name tag, that doesn't match.

Anticipate questions the editor might have when reviewing your report, and deal with them. If you said the employee wasn't wearing a name tag, then refer to her by name, tell how you got her name.

Include all relevant details. Editors have told me that they have never said to a shopper, "You give too many details." But don't include unnecessary details that don't add to the report.

Don't allow one aspect of your visit to affect the entire shop report. Shoppers sometimes latch onto one thing, and mention it repeatedly in the report. For example, if the fork you received had dried food on it, mention it in the appropriate section. But don't keep coming back to it, such as, "The food was probably good, but I lost my appetite when I received a dirty fork," and "Although the service was attentive, I rated it poor because they should have noticed that my fork was not clean."

Keep your writing professional. Don't end many (or perhaps any) sentences with exclamation points, and never use multiple exclamation points!!! Don't use "cute" language or emoticons, such as ;o).

Proofread carefully for correct spelling, grammar and punctuation. Make your report the best it can be.

Getting Paid

Payment procedures are explained when you are accepted as a contract shopper, or in the guidelines you receive for the shop. Some mystery shopping companies will pay you automatically based on your submission of a completed report and receipt or other documentation. Others want you to submit an invoice along with the report. The mystery shopping company can not invoice the client without complete information from you, so you won't be paid if you don't submit a complete report, receipt and any other documentation required for the shop.

If you do not complete the shop as instructed, and within the time required you may not be paid (or your pay could be reduced). Going on the wrong date, not spending enough time at the location, failing to follow the scenario, and other errors mean that the client will not accept your shop report. The mystery shopping company won't be paid for that report and they probably will not pay you.

Fortunately, all of these errors are easy to avoid. When you simply follow the guidelines you are given, do the shop as required, and submit a complete report before the deadline you shouldn't have any problems.

Some companies will reduce your pay if they have to call you about an incomplete report or extensive editing is required. Others will pay a bonus when you do excellent work and submit reports promptly. All of this will be explained when you receive your assignment.

Once you have submitted your report, you will be paid during the company's usual pay cycle. That could mean you get paid in a few days, a few weeks or the following month. The company will tell you their pay cycle when you apply or when you accept an assignment. Typically, you will be paid within three to six weeks of completing the shop, with some payments coming sooner, a few later.

Most companies pay by check. Some now offer direct deposit to your bank account.

Many companies are now using PayPal to pay shoppers, and the trend is that more companies seem to be using PayPal. If a company makes payments via PayPal, you will be notified at the time you apply.

PayPal is an online payment system. If you buy or sell on eBay, you may already be familiar with it. To set up an account, go to http://www.PayPal.com/. You will need to specify an e-mail account when you establish your PayPal account. Make sure that the e-mail address you give the mystery shopping companies is the same one you use with PayPal. The e-mail address is what will get the payments to your account. You may have more than one e-mail address attached to your PayPal account, so if you already have an account and want to add a mystery shopping e-mail address, you may add it to your current account.

Personal accounts are free, and you won't be charged to receive funds. You can have the money in your PayPal account transferred to your bank account, you can use it to make a purchase from a merchant who accepts PayPal, you can use a PayPal debit card to spend it or withdraw it through an ATM, or you can ask for a check. There may be fees involved with some of these transactions; however, it is free to have the money deposited in your bank account.

It is a good idea to keep a record of the shops you do for each mystery shopping company, the fees and reimbursements due, and the dates services were rendered. Record the payment when it is received.

By recording your shops and payments in this way you will always know exactly how much you are owed, or if the account is paid in full. Once in a while something happens to a check (e.g., your paperwork is misplaced, the check goes astray in the mail, etc.) and you want to make sure you receive all of your pay.

You can use a spreadsheet, such as *The Mystery Shopping Bible,* or a database or accounting program on your computer to keep track of your fees. This will also simplify pulling together the information you need for your tax return.

Payment Issues

What should you do when you don't receive an expected payment from a mystery shopping company? The first thing you should do is verify the company's pay cycle. If they say they pay on the 15th of the month following the shop, don't expect that you will open your mailbox on the 15th and find a check. Allow seven to ten days for the check to be cut and mailed, and for it to reach you. Even if payment is made via PayPal, it may be a few days after the payment date before the money shows up in your account.

Once you know that you should have received the payment by now, contact your scheduler or other company contact and ask the status. Remember that they are dealing with a large volume of e-mails, and they will probably have to check with someone else to get the answer for you. Allow at least a day or two for a response.

If you don't receive a response, or you don't receive a satisfactory response, take your request to the next level. Go the to mystery shopping company's web site, and look for contact information. E-mail or call to ask about the payment due you.

In all of the years I have been mystery shopping, I have never had a problem being paid. However, at times it does happen. If your shop was invalid because you did not follow instructions, you may not be paid. There have been a few instances where companies, due to financial difficulties or other issues, did not pay shoppers on schedule. If the company is a member of the MSPA, you can file a complaint with the MSPA for non-payment. Whether or not the company is an MSPA member, you may be able to file a complaint with the Better Business Bureau or even file suit in small claims court.

It is not wise to post a complaint about a company to a public forum, such as Volition.com, at least until you have made reasonable attempts to collect. Making false accusations against a company will not be good for your reputation. Be patient if a company is in communication and appears to be working with you. It can take time to investigate a problem, and things do get lost in the mail. Before posting, you may wish to e-mail ray@volition.com. He may be aware of other shoppers in the same situation, or may be able to offer advice.

Pet Peeves of
Mystery Shopping Companies

Want to know how to annoy mystery shopping companies? These were their most commonly mentioned pet peeves:

Not reading and following shop guidelines.

Accepting assignments, then disappearing and not completing them.

Not communicating questions or problems.

Inconsistency in report answers and comments.

Rushing through shops and reports.

Poor grammar and spelling.

Not telling the truth.

Failing to admit mistakes.

Submitting late reports.

Working with Mystery Shopping Companies

Once you start receiving assignments you will want to do the best job you can so that companies continue to send you mystery shopping opportunities, and perhaps increase the number of shops you are offered.

When you do a good job, companies will happily offer you more work if they can. The mystery shopping companies I surveyed all said that they have shoppers they employ as often as possible because they are dependable and do excellent work. There are also shoppers they would love to give more assignments to, but they simply don't have enough clients in the shopper's area to do so. And, of course, there are shoppers they won't work with again because they didn't do the shop they were given.

Even though some companies may not be able to work with you as much as you and they would like, you will probably find that there are a least a couple of companies that have a large number of shops available in your area. Doing your best work will keep them sending you all the assignments they can.

Doing Your Best

The three most important things to remember about doing a mystery shop are:

> Do it on time.
> Do it completely.
> Do it accurately.

On time means that the shop is completed and your report submitted by (or before) the deadline.

Completely means that you have provided all required information, filled in all of the spaces on the form, and made appropriate comments. Also remember to submit any required documentation, such as a receipt.

Accurately means that the shop was done on the correct day and at the proper time, the information you provided is correct, the ratings correlate with your comments, and the report is the best work you can possibly do.

The fourth and most important point: *do it.* If you accept, but do not complete an assignment, it is likely that you will not receive another assignment from that company. If an emergency comes up that keeps you from completing your assignment, or keeps you from getting your report in on time, call the company immediately to let them know.

Dos and Don'ts

Following these suggestions will keep you in good graces with mystery shopping companies and schedulers, and will help you go to the front of the line for more and better assignments.

Do communicate with the mystery shopping companies you work with and let them know about anything that will affect getting your reports done on time.

Don't call them just to chat. They don't have time.

Do drop them an e-mail to let them know if there has been a change in your contact information or availability.

Don't badger them about when they will have a shop for you, or why they don't give you more assignments. That's a sure way to get no assignments in the future!

Do complete your assignments as soon as possible during the shopping period.

Don't ask for extra time to complete your assignments, time after time.

Do respond promptly when a mystery shopping company contacts you with an assignment or a question.

Don't let phone messages and e-mail pile up.

Do be willing to take on a last minute assignment, or go a little out of your way to do a shop when the mystery shopping company is in a crunch.

Don't cause a crunch by canceling at the last minute or failing to do a shop you accepted.

Do turn in complete reports and any receipts or other required documentation.

Don't submit incomplete information that causes the company to have to call you.

And always remember to be polite and considerate. The people at mystery shopping companies are just that—people. They have good days and bad days, and they have to deal with stress, just like you. Be courteous and cooperative when you work with them and help make their jobs a little easier. They will remember you as a shopper with whom they enjoy working.

Dealing with Problems

You accepted the shop, but now you can't do it, or you can't do it on time. Perhaps you did the shop but you forgot to get a business card from the employee you spoke with. Or you lost the receipt. Or your computer crashed and you can't complete the report. What should you do?

First of all, contact the mystery shopping company or scheduler by e-mail or phone to let them know about the problem. Tell them what you can and can't do, then let them decide how to handle the situation.

When you can't do a shop you've accepted because of an emergency, they will reschedule it with another shopper. By telling them as soon as possible, you give them time to get it done.

Don't ask someone else to do the shop in your place. The mystery shopping company contracted with you, and your shop usually can not be assigned to someone else. However, if you know someone who could fill in for you, you may suggest them to the mystery shopping company.

If you can't make a deadline, the company may be able to extend it by a day or two. Don't rely on this month after month, but in a real emergency they can probably work with you. I once had to do this because of car trouble on the day the shop was scheduled. I immediately called the mystery shopping company, let them know about the problem and that I was getting the car fixed that day. I offered to do the shop first thing the following morning and get the report to them immediately afterward. They were understanding and allowed me to do the shop the next day. Had I not called, and waited for them to call me asking for the report, they would not have been as understanding.

You may be required to submit a receipt or business card from the shop along with your report. If something happened to it, or you forgot to get it, contact the company and ask how they want to handle it. Don't just submit the report without the receipt and hope they don't notice. They will. Be honest and up front with them and you may be able to salvage the situation.

Many reports are now done on the computer in Word or Excel, or via the Internet, so a computer crash can be a real problem. When reports are done on the web, you can access the Internet through another computer (such as a friend's or one at the library) and complete your report that way. If the report forms crashed with your computer, contact the company and ask what they want you to do.

Bottom line: Whenever there is a problem, contact the mystery shopping company or scheduler, let them know what happened and let them decide what should be done. If you can offer a solution, do so; but they will decide how it will be handled.

Avoiding Problems

Stuff happens, and anyone can make a mistake or have an emergency pop up. Although companies will be understanding in an emergency, if you seem to have a problem on every assignment the assignments will stop coming. A few simple steps can help you to avoid the situations described above.

Keep good records of your assignments, so you know what is due and when. "I forgot" is not considered a valid excuse for missing a deadline.

When scheduling shops, remember your other commitments. One shopper canceled an assignment at the last minute saying she "forgot Christmas was in December." Not good.

Do your shops early. When you have a window of time to complete the assignment, plan to do the shop as early as possible. That way, if something goes wrong you still have time to get it done by the deadline.

Review all instructions and requirements carefully before doing the shop to minimize the possibility of forgetting to do part of the evaluation, or not getting documentation you need, such as a receipt or business card.

Write the report as soon as you finish the shop, and send receipts immediately, before you have a chance to lose them.

Back up your computer files regularly so that if you have a crash you can get up and running quickly.

Have contingency plans in place. Think about the "what ifs" and come up with solutions you can implement if they become reality.

E-mail Tips

Many of your dealings with mystery shopping companies will be via e-mail. If your e-mails are well-written and professional, they enhance your professional image and help you to succeed. Here are some tips to make your e-mails more effective.

You may want a separate e-mail address just for mystery shopping. It can make it easier to manage your shopping e-mail.

E-mail is available from your ISP (e.g., AOL, Earthlink, etc.) and from free services (e.g., Yahoo, Hotmail, etc.). You may also have e-mail with any web sites you own (e.g., my e-mail is cathy@idealady.com, because IdeaLady.com is one of my web sites).

Free services may have limitations on how many e-mails can be in your inbox, the size of attachments you may receive, and more. Be certain you can live with any limitations.

Chose an e-mail address that you will have for a long time. When it changes, you will have to update your contact information at each company you are registered with. If your e-mail is through your ISP, your e-mail will change if you change ISPs.

If you use anti-spam software, make sure your mystery shopping e-mails will make it through. Some require senders to click a link and enter a code for their e-mail to be delivered. Automated e-mails sent by mystery shopping companies won't get to you.

Get good anti-virus software. If your machine becomes infected, it may become a problem for anyone and everyone in your address book and inbox.

Don't send attachments unless they are expected (e.g., completed reports, receipts, etc.).

Keep it simple. Don't use lots of graphics and HTML code in your e-mails. What looks like an adorable graphic to you may simply be garbage text in some e-mail software. Don't use odd fonts and unreadable colors.

When corresponding about a shop, provide all relevant information: your name, the client and location, assignment number, etc.

Respond promptly when a response is expected. If you are asked to confirm an assignment, do so promptly.

Don't put schedulers on your joke list, don't send them the latest virus warnings, and don't solicit cash for your charity. They don't want to receive that cute little movie, or pictures from your recent vacation.

Find the Errors in this E-mail:

Date: Mon, 10 Jan 2005
From: jill98356789@hotmail.com
To: scheduler@mysteryshoppingcompany.com
Subject:

I applied and gets no josb from you. Whats up????

jill

Where to begin? There are so many errors in such a short e-mail:

This is a poor choice of e-mail address. Lots of numbers in the e-mail address will cause many spam filters to think this is spam.

There is no subject, so we don't know what the e-mail is about. Of course, even after reading it, we're not sure what this e-mail is about.

"Gets" should be "get," "jobs" is misspelled, "What's" is missing the apostrophe, and what's up with all those question marks???? "Jill" should be capitalized. Hmmmm . . . I think we're starting to understand why "jill gets no josb."

There should be more than a first name. Include your full name and other identifiers, including your phone number, city and where you shop.

It turns out that this e-mail address is not the same one Jill used when she applied, so the mystery shopping company has no idea who she is, where she is, when she applied or even if she submitted an application.

A Better E-Mail:

Date: Mon, 10 Jan 2005
From: JillShops@hotmail.com
To: scheduler@mysteryshoppingcompany.com
Subject: Shopper Update: Certification Status

I applied to your company in September, 2004, but have not had the opportunity to complete any assignments for you. This weekend I obtained MSPA Gold Certification, and have updated my profile at your web site.

Please keep me in mind when you have assignments available in Northwest Houston and Harris County. I have shopped for many other companies, and consistently receive high ratings on my reports. I would love to have the chance to show you what I can do for you.

I am available for last-minute shops when you have a cancellation. I can be contacted by e-mail or at either of the phone numbers below.

Thank you. I am looking forward to working with you soon.

Jill McGillicutty
Houston, TX - Shopping NW Houston, Spring, Tomball, Conroe, and The Woodlands
MSPA Gold Certified
(281) 555-1234 / (281) 555-5678 (mobile)

This e-mail won't guarantee Jill any assignments, but it is more likely to work than the previous example.

Should You Start Your Own Mystery Shopping Company?

After you've been mystery shopping for a while, you may decide that you want to start a mystery shopping business of your own. One obvious advantage is that you may be able to make more money in a business of your own than when you are shopping as a contractor for someone else. Of course, like any other business, starting a mystery shopping company comes with cost and risk.

The things you enjoy about mystery shopping can make you a good candidate to start your own mystery shopping business. The best mystery shoppers are those who value excellent customer service and are passionate about providing information that helps businesses improve and become more successful.

On the other hand, there is a big difference between doing mystery shops and running a mystery shopping company. As the business owner you are responsible for selling your service to clients, selecting and managing shoppers, making sure reports are all completed on time, reviewing and editing the reports, submitting data to clients, invoicing clients, paying shoppers and more. You may find that you miss the days of being "just a shopper."

Many of today's successful mystery shopping companies were started by people just like you. After you've weighed all the pros and cons, you may decide that mystery shopping is the business for you. If so, here are some tips to get started.

It helps if you have experience in a customer service industry, such as retail or hospitality. Not only will you know what is required to deliver great service in those industries, you probably have contacts you can use to get your first clients. Perhaps a company you used to work for would like to hire you to mystery shop them.

General business and management experience is useful. As the business owner, you will have to manage staff, oversee collections and financial issues, train new shoppers, and use other skills you honed as a supervisor or manager.

Make sure you didn't sign a non-compete agreement with any of the mystery shopping companies you've worked for. This type of agreement (or it may be a clause in your independent contractor agreement) says that you can not start your own mystery shopping company while you are working for them, and often for a period of one year after you no longer work for them.

If you have signed any non-compete agreements, immediately ask those companies to remove you from their shopper databases. You would be wise to consult an attorney regarding when you may start your own business after giving such notice.

Don't violate the confidentiality agreements you signed with other mystery shopping companies by copying their report forms, applications, contracts, training manuals, web sites or other proprietary information.

Your independent contractor agreements may prohibit you from approaching companies you mystery shopped as a contractor. When in doubt, consult with an attorney.

You can begin your business part time, but make sure you are available to clients when they need you. Check messages frequently, or use a voice mail system that pages you when messages are received, so you can respond quickly to calls.

Because you will be going to your clients, and your clients won't be coming to you, you can start the business from your home. You will want a separate phone line to use for business, and you may want an address other than your home address to use for business. It is inexpensive to rent a post office box or private mail box.

Many executive suites have business identity programs. These programs allow you to use their mailing address and provide access to other services. You can have your phone line directed to them so your phone is always answered during business hours, they often have secretarial and administrative services available, and they have offices and conference rooms that you can rent as needed.

Don't try to be all things to all people. Your business may expand to cover all types of evaluations, but at the beginning you may want to specialize in an industry where you have experience.

Pricing can be tricky. Your service doesn't have to be the cheapest to get customers. In fact, setting prices too low can cost you customers. If you don't value your service, why should potential customers?

Many new business owners make the mistake of underpricing because they don't consider all the costs of doing business. Remember that it's not just the direct costs and your time to do a shop. You have overhead expenses (such as rent, phone lines, a web site, etc.), marketing expenses, and as you grow you will have to pay shoppers, schedulers and editors, and other staff.

Get help. General business assistance is available from the Small Business Administration and other agencies. They can help you with start up issues, marketing and more.

Consult with an attorney when drafting legal documents such as client contracts, independent contractor agreements, etc.

Build a network of shoppers right from the start, or work with someone (such as an independent scheduler) who already has a database of shoppers. You can't do every shop yourself, both because you won't have the time to do all of the shops plus everything else you have to do, and because your clients want observations by people other than you. Most clients don't want the same shopper evaluating the business any more often than every three months.

To learn more about the industry, attend the semi-annual educational conferences sponsored by the Mystery Shopping Providers Association <http://www.mysteryshop.org>. You will get to know the people at many other mystery shopping companies, and you will have the opportunity to learn from their experience. Your "competition" may be your greatest asset in starting your new business.

Appendix A:
Mystery Shopping
Directory

This section includes contact information for companies that hire mystery shoppers, including mystery shopping companies, schedulers and businesses that hire mystery shoppers directly. These companies have sites on the Internet, and most of them allow you to make your application online. In fact, most prefer or require that you apply online.

To jump start your mystery shopping career, sit at the computer with this list and start making applications to the companies that most interest you. You won't always know which companies need shoppers in your area, and companies' needs change over time. To get started quickly and make yourself eligible for more assignments, apply to many companies. Start out by applying to at least 20 companies, and apply to a few more from time to time. If you've done the preparation recommended in the Quick-Start Plan on page 77, you should be able to submit 20, 30 or more applications in a single evening at the computer.

Pay attention to the information at each web site. If a company wants experienced shoppers, don't apply until you have experience. If they have any requirement you don't meet, don't waste your time and theirs by submitting an application.

We have included the location of each company, but you shouldn't apply only to companies that are in your geographic area. Even companies that are not located in your area may have clients near you, and that is what matters.

This list is presented for your information, and the inclusion of a company on this list does not imply a recommendation of that company.

We have attempted to include only companies which do not require an application fee or other charges for accepting you as a mystery shopper, or at least to note any charges we were aware of.

The listing for each company includes space for you to note the date you applied, your Log-in or Shopper ID, Password and Notes about the company.

This company list was current as we went to press; however, the business changes rapidly, so expect that some companies will change their hiring practices and others will change name, web site or physical address, or go out of business.

If you are unable to reach a company's web site through the URL listed here, there are several possible reasons. It may be that the web site is temporarily unavailable, so try it again later. The URL may have changed, so you might try doing a search for the company name at Google.com or other search engines. Of course, it is also possible that the company is no longer in business or they are doing business under another name.

If you've gone through this list and still want more, there are many other companies that do mystery shopping. Review the information on How to Find More Companies in Appendix B to locate additional mystery shopping companies (including companies operating locally).

A Closer Look
Norcross, GA
http://www.a-closer-look.com/
Date applied: _____
Log-in: _____ Password: _____
Notes: _____

A Customer's Point of View, Inc.
Stockbridge, GA
http://www.acpview.com/
Date applied: _____
Log-in: _____ Password: _____
Notes: _____

A Top Shop!
Littleton, CO
http://www.atopshop.com/
Date applied: _____
Log-in: _____ Password: _____
Notes: _____

ACE Mystery Shopping
Sedalia, MO
http://acemysteryshopping.com/
Date applied: _____
Log-in: _____ Password: _____
Notes: _____

ACRA, Inc.
Mantua, NJ
http://www.acra.us/
Date applied: _____
Log-in: _____ Password: _____
Notes: _____

AIM Field Service
Apopka, FL
http://www.patsaim.com/
Date applied: _____
Log-in: _____ Password: _____
Notes: _____

Alexandria's Marketing Company
Granger, IL
http://www.alexandriasmarketing.com/
Primarily merchandising and demos
Date applied: _____
Log-in: _____ Password: _____
Notes: _____

A & M Business Services
Pensacola, FL
http://www.ambussvcs.com/
Date applied: _____
Log-in: _____ Password: _____
Notes: _____

Amusement Advantage, LLC
Arvada, CO
http://www.amusementadvantage.com/
Date applied: _____
Log-in: _____ Password: _____
Notes: _____

Ann Michaels & Associates, Ltd.
Naperville, IL
http://www.annmichaelsltd.com/
Date applied: _____
Log-in: _____ Password: _____
Notes: _____

Anonymous Insights Inc
Dublin, OH
http://www.a-insights.com/
Date applied: _____
Log-in: _____ Password: _____
Notes: _____

At Your Service Marketing
Chico, TX
http://www.aysm.com/
Regional merchandising and MS
Date applied: _____
Log-in: _____ Password: _____
Notes: _____

Ath Power Consulting Corporation
Andover, MA
http://athpower.com/
Date applied: _____
Log-in: _____ Password: _____
Notes: _____

Athena Research Group, Inc.
Riverside, CA
http://www.athenamarketresearch.com/
Date applied: _____
Log-in: _____ Password: _____
Notes: _____

BanConsult, Inc.
Okemos, MI
http://www.banconsult.com/
Date applied: _____
Log-in: _____ Password: _____
Notes: _____

Bare Associates International Inc.
Fairfax, VA
http://www.baiservices.com/
Date applied: _____
Log-in: _____ Password: _____
Notes: _____

Barry Leeds & Associates Inc.
    Div of Informa Research Services
New York, NY
http://www.BarryLeedsassoc.com/
Date applied: _____
Log-in: _____   Password: _____
Notes: _____

BestMark
Minnetonka, MN
http://www.bestmark.com/
Date applied: _____
Log-in: _____   Password: _____
Notes: _____

Beyond Hello Inc
Madison, WI
http://www.beyondhello.com/
Date applied: _____
Log-in: _____   Password: _____
Notes: _____

BLD Scheduling Services
Las Vegas, NV
http://www.BLDSchedulers.com/
Date applied: _____
Log-in: _____   Password: _____
Notes: _____

BMA-Best Market Audits, Inc.
Spring City, PA
http://www.mystery-shopping.com/
Date applied: _____
Log-in: _____ Password: _____
Notes: _____

Brand Marketing International
Sarasota, FL
http://www.bmiltd.com/
Date applied: _____
Log-in: _____ Password: _____
Notes: _____

Business Evaluation Services
Bakersfield, CA
http://www.mysteryshopperservices.com/
Date applied: _____
Log-in: _____ Password: _____
Notes: _____

Capstone Research Inc.
Fairfield, NJ
http://www.capstoneresearch.com/
Date applied: _____
Log-in: _____ Password: _____
Notes: _____

Certified Reports, Inc.
Kinderhook, NY
http://www.certifiedreports.com/
Date applied: _____
Log-in: _____ Password: _____
Notes: _____

CheckMark, Inc.
Batavia, OH
http://www.checkmarkinc.com/
Date applied: _____
Log-in: _____ Password: _____
Notes: _____

Cirrus Marketing Consultants
Anaheim, CA
http://www.cirrusmktg.com/
Date applied: _____
Log-in: _____ Password: _____
Notes: _____

Coast to Coast Scheduling Services
La Mirada, CA
http://www.ctcss.com/
Date applied: _____
Log-in: _____ Password: _____
Notes: _____

Confero Inc
Cary, NC
http://www.conferoinc.com/
Date applied: _____
Log-in: _____ Password: _____
Notes: _____

Corporate Research Group
Nepean, ON
http://www.thecrg.com/
Date applied: _____
Log-in: _____ Password: _____
Notes: _____

Creative Image Associates, Inc.
Lunenburg, MA
http://www.creativeimage.net/
Date applied: _____
Log-in: _____ Password: _____
Notes: _____

Cross Financial Group
Lincoln, NE
http://www.crossfinancial.com/
Date applied: _____
Log-in: _____ Password: _____
Notes: _____

Customer 1st
Greensboro, NC
http://www.customer-1st.com/
Date applied: _____
Log-in: _____ Password: _____
Notes: _____

Customer Perspectives
Hooksett, NH
http://www.customerperspectives.com/
Date applied: _____
Log-in: _____ Password: _____
Notes: _____

Customer Service Experts, Inc.
Annapolis, MD
http://www.customerserviceexperts.com/
Date applied: _____
Log-in: _____ Password: _____
Notes: _____

Customer Service Profiles
Omaha, NE
http://www.csprofiles.com/
Date applied: _____
Log-in: _____ Password: _____
Notes: _____

CV Marketing Research Inc.
Abbotsford, BC
http://www.cv-market.com/
http://www.cv-mystery.com/
Date applied: _____
Log-in: _____ Password: _____
Notes: _____

Data Quest, Ltd.
Boston, MA
http://www.dataquestonline.com/
Date applied: _____
Log-in: _____ Password: _____
Notes: _____

David Sparks & Associates
Clemson, SC
http://www.sparksresearch.com/
Date applied: _____
Log-in: _____ Password: _____
Notes: _____

Devon Hill Associates
La Jolla, CA
http://www.devonhillassociates.com/
Date applied: _____
Log-in: _____ Password: _____
Notes: _____

DSG Associates Inc
Santa Ana, CA
http://www.dsgai.com/
Date applied: _____
Log-in: _____ Password: _____
Notes: _____

Ellis Property Management Services
Irving, TX
http://www.epmsonline.com/
Date applied: _____
Log-in: _____ Password: _____
Notes: _____

Feedback Plus, Inc.
Dallas, TX
http://www.feedbackplusinc.com/
Date applied: _____
Log-in: _____ Password: _____
Notes: _____

Focus On Service LLC
Hopkinton, MA
http://www.focusonservice.com/
Date applied: _____
Log-in: _____ Password: _____
Notes: _____

G3 Mystery Shopping
Sylvania, Ohio
http://www.g3mysteryshopping.com/
Date applied: _____
Log-in: _____ Password: _____
Notes: _____

Game Film/Mystery Shoppers, Inc.
Austin, TX
http://www.gamefilmconsultants.com/
Date applied: _____
Log-in: _____ Password: _____
Notes: _____

Global Compliance Services
        (formerly Pinkerton Reasearch)
Charlotte, NC
http://www.pktnshop.com/
Date applied: _____
Log-in: _____ Password: _____
Notes: _____

HR and Associates
Clarendon Hills, IL
http://www.hrandassociates.com/
Date applied: _____
Log-in: _____ Password: _____
Notes: _____

ICC Decision Services
Wayne, NJ
http://www.iccds.com/
Date applied: _____
Log-in: _____ Password: _____
Notes: _____

Infotel, Inc.
Los Gatos, CA
http://www.infotelinc.com/
Date applied: _____
Log-in: _____ Password: _____
Notes: _____

IntelliShop
Perrysburg, OH
http://www.intelli-shop.com/
Date applied: _____
Log-in: _____ Password: _____
Notes: _____

Ipsos-Insight
Houston, TX
http://www.ipsos-insight.com/
Date applied: _____
Log-in: _____ Password: _____
Notes: _____

Jack In the Box, Inc.
San Diego, CA
http://www.jacksguest.com/
Date applied: _____
Log-in: _____ Password: _____
Notes: _____

Jancyn
San Jose, CA
http://www.jancyn.com/
Date applied: _____
Log-in: _____ Password: _____
Notes: _____

JM Ridgway
San Jose, CA
http://www.jmridgway.com/
Date applied: _____
Log-in: _____ Password: _____
Notes: _____

Kern Scheduling Services
Tucson, AZ
http://www.kernscheduling.com/
Date applied: _____
Log-in: _____ Password: _____
Notes: _____

Kinesis-CEM
Seattle, WA
http://www.kinesis-cem.com/
Date applied: _____
Log-in: _____ Password: _____
Notes: _____

Loews Theatres
http://www.enjoytheshow.com/mysteryshopper/
Charges a fee for specified benefits. See the web site.
Date applied: _____
Log-in: _____ Password: _____
Notes: _____

Maritz Research
Fenton, MO
http://www.maritzresearch.com/
Date applied: _____
Log-in: _____ Password: _____
Notes: _____

Marketing Endeavors, LLC
Louisville, KY
http://www.marketingendeavors.biz/
Date applied: _____
Log-in: _____ Password: _____
Notes: _____

Marketing Systems Unlimited Corp
Iowa City, IA
http://www.msultd.com/
Date applied: _____
Log-in: _____ Password: _____
Notes: _____

Marketwise Consulting Group, Inc.
Hortonville, WI
http://www.marketwi.com/
Date applied: _____
Log-in: _____ Password: _____
Notes: _____

Mars Research
Multiple locations.
http://www.marsresearch.com/
Date applied: _____
Log-in: _____ Password: _____
Notes: _____

MCG, Management Consultant Group, LLC
Metairie, LA
http://www.managementconsultantgroup.com/
Date applied: _____
Log-in: _____ Password: _____
Notes: _____

Mercantile Systems & Surveys
Brentwood, CA
http://www.mercsurveys.com/
Date applied: _____
Log-in: _____ Password: _____
Notes: _____

Michelson & Associates
Atlanta, GA
http://www.michelson.com/
Date applied: _____
Log-in: _____ Password: _____
Notes: _____

Mintel International Group Ltd.
Chicage, IL
http://www.services.mintel.com/
Date applied: _____
Log-in: _____ Password: _____
Notes: _____

Mystery Guest, Inc.
Winter Park, FL
http://www.mysteryguestinc.com/
Date applied: _____
Log-in: _____ Password: _____
Notes: _____

Mystery Shoppers
Knoxville, TN
http://mystery-shoppers.com/
Date applied: _____
Log-in: _____ Password: _____
Notes: _____

Mystery Shopping Solutions, Inc.
Tyngsboro, MA
http://www.mystshopsol.com/
Date applied: _____
Log-in: _____ Password: _____
Notes: _____

Mystique Shopper LLC
Clermont, FL
http://www.mystiqueshopper.com/
Date applied: _____
Log-in: _____ Password: _____
Notes: _____

National Shopping Service
Rocklin, CA
http://www.nationalshoppingservice.com/
Date applied: _____
Log-in: _____ Password: _____
Notes: _____

National Shopping Service Network
http://www.mysteryshopper.net/
Date applied: _____
Log-in: _____ Password: _____
Notes: _____

Nationwide Services Group, Inc.
Cleveland, OH
http://www.nationwidesg.com/
Date applied: _____
Log-in: _____ Password: _____
Notes: _____

NOP World Mystery Shopping
New York, NY
http://www.ropernopmysteryshopping.com/
Date applied: _____
Log-in: _____ Password: _____
Notes: _____

People Plus Inc
Memphis, TN
http://www.peopleplusinc.net/
Date applied: _____
Log-in: _____ Password: _____
Notes: _____

Person to Person Quality
Alexandria, VA
http://persontopersonquality.com/
Date applied: _____
Log-in: _____ Password: _____
Notes: _____

Personnel Profiles, Inc.
Boulder, CO
http://www.ppiadvantage.com/
Date applied: _____
Log-in: _____ Password: _____
Notes: _____

Professional Review & Operational Shoppers, Inc.
Vero Beach, FL
http://www.proreview.com/
Date applied: _____
Log-in: _____ Password: _____
Notes: _____

Promotion Network, Inc.
Palos Heights, IL
http://www.PromotionNetworkInc.com/
Date applied: _____
Log-in: _____ Password: _____
Notes: _____

Pulseback, Inc.
Manchester, VT
http://www.pulseback.com/
Date applied: _____
Log-in: _____ Password: _____
Notes: _____

QSI Specialists
Las Vegas, NV
http://www.globalintelligence.net/
Date applied: _____
Log-in: _____ Password: _____
Notes: _____

Quality Assessments Mystery Shoppers
Springfield, IL
http://www.qams.com/
Date applied: _____
Log-in: _____ Password: _____
Notes: _____

Quest for Best/Quest Associates Inc.
Memphis, TN
http://www.questforbest.com/
Date applied: _____
Log-in: _____ Password: _____
Notes: _____

Reality Check
Seattle, WA
http://www.rcmysteryshopper.com/
Date applied: _____
Log-in: _____ Password: _____
Notes: _____

Resort Loyalty, Inc.
Breckenridge, CO
http://www.resortloyalty.com/
Date applied: _____
Log-in: _____ Password: _____
Notes: _____

Restaurant Evaluators, Inc.
Chicago, IL
http://www.restaurantevaluators.com/
Date applied: _____
Log-in: _____ Password: _____
Notes: _____

Ritter & Associates
Toledo, OH
http://www.ritterandassociates.com/
Date applied: _____
Log-in: _____ Password: _____
Notes: _____

Rocky Mountain Research
Salt Lake City, UT
http://www.rockymm.com/
Date applied: _____
Log-in: _____   Password: _____
Notes: _____

RQA, Inc.
Phoenix, AZ
http://www.rqa-inc.com/
Date applied: _____
Log-in: _____   Password: _____
Notes: _____

Safeguard Services, Inc.
Honolulu, HI
http://www.safeguardhawaii.com/
Date applied: _____
Log-in: _____   Password: _____
Notes: _____

Second To None Inc
Ann Arbor, MI
http://www.second-to-none.com/
Date applied: _____
Log-in: _____   Password: _____
Notes: _____

Secret Shopper - Sights on Service
Golden Valley, MN
http://www.secretshopper.com/
Date applied: _____
Log-in: _____ Password: _____
Notes: _____

Sensors Quality Management, Inc.
Toronto, ON
http://www.sqm.ca/
Date applied: _____
Log-in: _____ Password: _____
Notes: _____

Service Advantage International
Newport Beach, CA
http://www.servad.com/
Date applied: _____
Log-in: _____ Password: _____
Notes: _____

Service Alliance Inc
Aurora, CO
http://www.servicealllianceinc.com/
Date applied: _____
Log-in: _____ Password: _____
Notes: _____

Service Evaluation Concepts Inc
Woodbury, NY
http://www.serviceevaluation.com/
Date applied: _____
Log-in: _____ Password: _____
Notes: _____

Service Excellence Group Inc
St. Louis, MO
http://www.serviceexcellencegroup.com/
Date applied: _____
Log-in: _____ Password: _____
Notes: _____

Service Excellence Group
Reston, VA
http://www.mysteryshopsplus.com/
Date applied: _____
Log-in: _____ Password: _____
Notes: _____

Service Impressions
Lafayette, CA
http://www.serviceimpressions.com/
Date applied: _____
Log-in: _____ Password: _____
Notes: _____

Service Intelligence
Suwanee, GA / Calgary, AB
http://www.serviceintelligence.com/
Date applied: _____
Log-in: _____ Password: _____
Notes: _____

Service Performance Group Inc
Holly Springs, NC
http://www.spgweb.com/
Date applied: _____
Log-in: _____ Password: _____
Notes: _____

Service Sleuths/Howard Services
Franklin, MA
http://www.servicesleuths.com/
Date applied: _____
Log-in: _____ Password: _____
Notes: _____

ServiceProbe
Signal Mountain, TN
http://www.pwgroup.com/sprobe/
Date applied: _____
Log-in: _____ Password: _____
Notes: _____

ServiceSense
Nowell, MA
http://www.servicesense.com/
Date applied: _____
Log-in: _____ Password: _____
Notes: _____

SG Marketing Group
Arnold, CA
http://www.sgmarketing.com/
Date applied: _____
Log-in: _____ Password: _____
Notes: _____

Shop'n Chek Inc, *Worldwide
Norcross, GA
http://www.shopnchek.com/
Date applied: _____
Log-in: _____ Password: _____
Notes: _____

Shoppers Critique International LLC
Longwood, FL
http://www.shopperscritique.com/
Date applied: _____
Log-in: _____ Password: _____
Notes: _____

Shoppers' View
Grand Rapids, MI
http://www.shoppersview.com/
Date applied: _____
Log-in: _____ Password: _____
Notes: _____

Sinclair Service Assessments Inc
San Antonio, TX
http://www.ssanet.com/
Date applied: _____
Log-in: _____ Password: _____
Notes: _____

Speedmark Information Services
The Woodlands, TX
http://www.speedmarkweb.com/
http://www.sassieshop.com/2green
Date applied: _____
Log-in: _____ Password: _____
Notes: _____

Sutter Perfomance Group
Palatine, IL
http://www.suttermarketing.com/
Date applied: _____
Log-in: _____ Password: _____
Notes: _____

Tenox Appraisal Systems
Oakville, ON
http://www.weshop4u.com/
Date applied: _____
Log-in: _____   Password: _____
Notes: _____

Testshopper.com
Columbia, MD
http://www.testshopper.com/
Date applied: _____
Log-in: _____   Password: _____
Notes: _____

Texas Shoppers Network Inc
Houston, TX
http://www.texasshoppersnetwork.com/
Date applied: _____
Log-in: _____   Password: _____
Notes: _____

The Pat Henry Group
Cleveland, OH
http://www.pathenry.com/
Date applied: _____
Log-in: _____   Password: _____
Notes: _____

The Performance Edge, Inc.
Pleasant Grove, UT
http://www.pedge.com/
Date applied: _____
Log-in: _____ Password: _____
Notes: _____

The Secret Shopper Company
Gainsville, GA
http://www.secretshoppercompany.com/
Date applied: _____
Log-in: _____ Password: _____
Notes: _____

The Shadow Agency Inc.-Newmark
N. Richland Hills, TX
http://www.theshadowagency.com/
Date applied: _____
Log-in: _____ Password: _____
Notes: _____

The Shadow Shopper of Georgia Inc
Cumming, GA
http://www.tssog.com/
Date applied: _____
Log-in: _____ Password: _____
Notes: _____

TNS
Atlanta, GA
http://www.intersearch.tnsofres.com/
Date applied: _____
Log-in: _____ Password: _____
Notes: _____

TrendSource
San Diego, CA
http://www.trendsource.com/
Date applied: _____
Log-in: _____ Password: _____
Notes: _____

Video Eyes
http://www.videoeyes.net/
Date applied: _____
Log-in: _____ Password: _____
Notes: _____

Westcoast Mystery Shopping
Delta, BC
http://www.westcoastmysteryshopping.com/
Date applied: _____
Log-in: _____ Password: _____
Notes: _____

International Companies

AB Bättre Affärer/Better Business
Stockholm SE
http://www.battreaffarer.com/

AQ Services
The Hague NL
http://www.aq-services.com/

Bare Associates International Inc.
http://www.baiservices.com/

Catalyst Marketing Communications Ltd.
Dublin 4 IE
http://www.catalyst-mc.com/

Cliente Mistério Consultants
Lisbon PT
http://www.cliente-misterio.com/

Concertare GmbH
Burscheid / Köln DE
http://www.concertare.de/

DMA-Research
Aarhus C DK
http://www.dma-research.com/

ESA Market Research Ltd. St.
Albans UK
http://www.esa.co.uk/

Hans Smith Training & Advies
Hilversum NL
http://www.mysteryguest-review.nl/

Hoed Mystery Shopping
Epping NSW
http://www.hoedholdings.com.au/

Hoffmann & Forcher Marketing Research
Vienna AT
http://members.eunet.at/hoffmann.forcher/

InCite Research & Marketing
Dubai Media City AE
http://www.incitemar.com/

International Service Check
Munich DE
http://www.internationalservicecheck.com/

MacPherson Mystery Shopping & Research Ltd.
Huddersfield UK
http://www.macphersonmysteryshopping.org.uk/

Martine Constant & Partners, Antwerpen
Antwerpen BE
http://www.martineconstant.com/

Motori Mentali
Roma IT
http://www.incentivespa.it/

NIKKEI Research Inc.
Tokyo JP
http://nikkeiresearch.com/

Palvelu Plus - Service Plus Oy/Ltd
Helsinki FI
http://www.serviceplus.fi/

PIG Services
UK
http://www.pigservices.co.uk/

Présence Mystery Shopping
Paris FR
http://www.presence.fr/

RAI Consultants Services Ltd.
Nicosia CY
http://www.rai.com.cy/

React Surveys
Cirencester UK
http://www.reactsurveys.com/

Research International
London UK
http://www.research-int.com/

Retail Reality b.v.
Zeewolde NL
http://www.retailreality.nl/

Société DMS (Dynamic Marketing Services)
Nanterre Cedex FR
http://www.dmsfrance.com/

Synovate UK
Kent UK
http://www.synovate.com/

TEMO
Stockholm SE
http://www.temo.se/

THINKSMART
Madrid ES
http://www.thinksmart.es/

Appendix B:
How to Find More
Mystery Shopping
Companies

The previous section contains contact information for many mystery shopping companies that hire shoppers across the country, or even around the world. There are also mystery shopping companies that only shop in a limited area—perhaps your city or state. In this section, you'll learn how to find those companies, as well as how to find more national and international companies.

To find mystery shopping companies in your area, check the Yellow Pages of your phone directory. If you have separate Yellow Pages directories for consumers and businesses, these companies will be in the business directory. Your phone book won't have a heading for "Mystery Shopping", so try looking under Shopping Services - Commercial or Shopping Services-Protective, Price Comparison.

You can find mystery shopping leads by talking to other mystery shoppers and exchanging information about shopping. You're saying, "But I don't know any mystery shoppers!" Chances are, you do. It has just never come up before, or you didn't pay attention when they mentioned it. When you are more aware of mystery shopping, suddenly you'll meet other shoppers at parties, your child's play group, all over.

When talking about mystery shopping with others, don't give out proprietary information. Don't talk about fees or specific shops, but it's acceptable to say that you have shopped for ABC Mystery Shoppers and to tell another shopper how to contact them.

You can exchange information with other shoppers by visiting message boards and joining e-mail lists on the Internet. See Appendix C to learn where the message boards and mailing lists are. These services are free.

Using the Internet

One of the best resources for locating mystery shopping companies is the Internet. Two good resources for locating mystery shopping companies and shops are Volition.com and the Mystery Shopping Providers Association at: http://www.mysteryshop.org/. You can search for shops in your state, or to find companies by region, industry served or the types of shops they do.

There are lists of mystery shopping companies available for free on several web sites. Remember that the saying, "You get what you pay for," is frequently true. These lists are often out of date and you may spend a lot of time trying to reach companies that no longer exist. Some of the mystery shopping companies they name only shop in a small, local area.

I contacted companies from one list and found that many of them were market research companies, but they do not mystery shop, have never mystery shopped, and have no future plans to mystery shop.

The list of companies in this book will get you off to a good start. If you decide you want to apply to more companies, or different companies, check the MSPA and Volition web sites, look for companies offline using the suggestions earlier in this chapter, or search for companies online using the techniques that follow.

What to Do If You Don't Have Internet Access

Even if you don't have a computer or Internet access at home, you can find companies and apply to them online. Some mystery shopping companies want you to have full time Internet access at home or at work, but most don't care how you get to the Internet, as long as you can get online when you need to contact them, download shop forms and instructions, and submit reports.

Many public and university libraries have Internet access available to the public without charge. Call your local libraries and ask if they have this service available. They may also have free orientation sessions to teach you how to use the computers and find what you are looking for on the Internet. If not, the librarians can assist you in getting started.

Your employer may allow personal use of company computers. Make sure you're not violating company policy before using an employer's equipment or Internet account.

Friends or family members who have computers and Internet accounts might let you use their computers to apply to and keep in touch with mystery shopping companies. This could be a good temporary solution until you get your own computer.

There are businesses that offer computer and Internet access at hourly rates. The cost will eat into your profits, but this is a solution if you don't have any other way.

Remember that many business expenses are tax deductible. That means that you may be able to deduct some or all of the cost of your computer, printer, Internet connection, etc. Consider using some of your mystery shopping income to pay for a computer and online service.

Searching the Web

Whether you are using your own Internet account, or accessing the Internet through a public terminal or that of a friend, here is what you should do once you are connected to the web:

There are many *search engines* available to help you find what you are looking for. A search engine is like an index to help you find what you're looking for in the vastness of the Internet. A few of the best-known search engines are Yahoo, Google, Alta Vista, and Lycos. The service you are using to connect to the Internet may have a list of search engines with hotlinks. When you move the cursor (the little arrow you move around the screen with the mouse) over a hotlink, the arrow will change to a pointing hand. This means that if you click the left mouse button, it will connect you to the site.

If you can't find a list of search engines, your best bet is to go directly to Google. The software you are using (called a browser) will have a place on the screen where you can type in the URL (address) of the site you want to go to. Usually it is a box near the top of the screen. Key in http://www.google.com/, then press <enter>.

When you get to Google, there will be a box on the screen where you enter the subject of the search. Type in "mystery shopping" then press the <enter> key or click on the <Search> button on the screen. (To click on something on your screen, move the mouse until the cursor is positioned over the thing you want to click on. Then, press the left mouse button.)

The list of entries you get will each have a hotlink which you can click on to visit the site. After visiting the site, click on the <Back> button on the screen until you get back to your list of sites at Google. Then, visit the next site, and so on.

You can run the same search on several other search engines. Each search engine will give you some different results. Try one or more of these:

http://www.yahoo.com/
http://www.altavista.com/
http://www.lycos.com/

Hints for Searching the Web

For best results when doing your search, search for "mystery shopper" or "mystery shopping." Searching for "mystery shop" will get more results; however, many of the pages you find will have nothing to do with mystery shopping. They will be for mystery bookshops, stores which sell Dungeons and Dragons materials, occult-related sites, etc.

Use quotation marks around your search term (e.g., "mystery shopping") to get better results. If you just type the two words, (e.g., mystery shopping) most search engines will give you a list of all the places that use either one of the words, not just the two words used together.

You will find many places offering to sell information about mystery shopping. Like every place else you can buy things, some are legitimate and some are not.

You will find sites with free lists of mystery shopping companies. I've checked out some of these lists and found some good information, but a lot of listings were out of date, incomplete, or include companies that operate only in a small local or regional area, or that don't do mystery shopping at all (and never have). So don't spend a lot of time trying to apply to lots of companies you found on a "free" list.

Be prepared before going online. Have your information ready to input. Follow the suggestions in the Quick-Start Plan on page 77.

When applying online, use common sense regarding what you disclose. Most of the people you encounter on the Internet are honest, but don't give out any information you wouldn't give someone who called you on the phone until you are certain of who you are dealing with.

One way you can check out a company before deciding if you will apply to them is to see if the company belongs to the MSPA. Member companies have agreed to uphold ethical standards, and MSPA member companies are legitimate. You can search for MSPA member companies in the shopper area of the web site at http://www.mysteryshop.org/.

Volition.com can also provide a lot of information about companies. Go to the mystery shopping forum, and search for the company name. If there are posts about the company, you can read them and learn about other shoppers' experiences.

Don't be overly influenced by one shopper's negative experience; however, if you see a pattern of problems with a company, you may choose not to work with them. After all, there are lots of other companies out there.

Appendix C:
Internet Resources

IdeaLady
http://www.IdeaLady.com/
http://www.mysteryshoppersmanual.com/
To keep up with new developments and updates on mystery shopping, visit the author's web sites. Be sure to sign up for the free e-mail course on mystery shopping.

Mystery Shopping Providers Association
http://www.mysteryshop.org/
A resource for mystery shoppers, mystery shopping companies, and businesses seeking mystery shopping services. Shoppers will find certification information, job postings, a message board, and links to mystery shopping companies around the world.

Volition.com

http://www.volition.com/mystery.html
Lots of links to mystery shopping companies, message boards, and other shopper resources. They also have links to information on merchandising and in-store demo jobs. The site has an active and informative message board and they host live chats regularly.

Message Boards

There are message boards, forums and e-mail discussion lists on the Internet where schedulers and mystery shopping companies post leads for mystery shopping and merchandising assignments. You may also be able to exchange information with other shoppers and learn more about mystery shopping.

Instructions for using these resources will be found at the sites listed. You may go to a web site to read or post messages, or some will allow you to have messages delivered directly to you via e-mail.

You will find several message boards, forums and discussion lists by searching for "mystery shopping," "secret shopping," and "merchandising" on these sites:

http://www.delphiforums.com/
http://lists.topica.com/
http://groups.yahoo.com/

National Association for Retail Marketing Services

http://www.narms.com/

For information about merchandising, demos, etc. You can complete an online profile that will be added to their database and made available to more than 250 member companies.

U.S. Internal Revenue Service

Tax information for U.S. shoppers

http://www.irs.gov/

Canada Revenue Agency

Tax information for Canadian Shoppers

http://www.cra-arc.gc.ca/

Grammar and Writing Resources

http://www.ccc.commnet.edu/grammar
http://www.dailygrammar.com/
http://www.chompchomp.com/
http://www.grammarlady.com/
http://www.m-w.com/ (Dictionary & Thesaurus)

Free Spell Check Program for Internet Explorer

http://www.iespell.com/

Tax and Legal Information for Independent Contractors

http://www.nolo.com/

Taping Laws

http://www.rcfp.org/taping

Private Investigator Laws

http://www.crimetime.com/licensing.htm

PayPal

http://www.paypal.com/

The Mystery Shopping Bible

http://www.yourwebness.com/

Appendix D:
Frequently Asked
Questions

Here are some of the questions many new shoppers ask about mystery shopping.

What is mystery shopping?
Mystery shoppers go into businesses as customers. They interact with employees, make a purchase and possibly a return, then fill out an evaluation form describing what happened during the visit. Mystery shoppers get paid for providing this service.

What kinds of businesses use mystery shoppers?
Any business which deals with the public may use mystery shoppers—stores, restaurants, banks, hotels, salons, home builders, apartment complexes, gas stations, casinos, auto dealers, auto service centers, movie theaters, health clubs, pet stores, amusement parks, optical providers and more. You can get paid to

get your hair cut or your eyes examined, have dinner, go to the bank, have your car worked on or fill up the gas tank, watch a movie, get your dog groomed, and lots of other things you like to (or have to) do.

How much will I earn?

That depends on you. Many shoppers do this in their spare time, and earn $300, $500, or more per month. Some consistently earn more—often a lot more. It is not unusual for a part time or spare time shopper to make $500 to $1000 or more per month.

Some shoppers work for a large number of companies, or are full time with one company, and make their living this way. It's not easy, though, to be a full time shopper. It will probably require that you work with a large number of mystery shopping companies—perhaps 50, 80 or more. You will have to juggle lots of assignments with different requirements, due dates and report formats, so you must be very organized and disciplined.

Fees for a mystery shop (including purchase reimbursement) may range from about $10 or $20 on up to $50, $100 or more. Fees will depend on the time required, difficulty, etc. The time required to complete a shop and fill out the form may be a few minutes to an hour or longer.

What are the requirements to be a mystery shopper?

You can be any (adult) age, male or female. You may be employed, self-employed, unemployed, a student, retired or a full time homemaker. You need to be observant and able to follow directions. You must be reliable. You don't have to have a degree or any special training or experience, although experience in customer service (such as having worked in hospitality or retail) is helpful. Writing skills are important, and you should have a good command of spelling, grammar and punctuation.

Companies often use the Internet to recruit shoppers, make assignments, and complete reports. Internet access is becoming a necessity to work with most mystery shopping companies, but there are still some which don't require it—especially some of the small, local companies.

How do I apply to be a mystery shopper?

In most cases, you won't be hired directly by the business you're mystery shopping. You'll be hired by a mystery shopping company contracted by the business.

Many mystery shopping companies now have applications at their web sites. That is the best way to apply. If you find a company that doesn't have an online application, the best way to apply is to send a one-page resume, a one-page letter of interest, and a self-addressed stamped envelope. DON'T CALL unless the company has said that it is OK to do so. Many of these companies have small staffs and they are dealing with hundreds or thousands of shoppers and assignments at a time. They don't have time to chat.

Are there jobs available in my area?

If you live in or regularly travel to an area where there are national or regional chain stores, banks, and restaurants there are certainly mystery shops being done there. Almost any business that does business with the public may be mystery shopped, although most "Mom and Pop"-type businesses don't use mystery shoppers.

New shoppers are being hired all the time as businesses begin new mystery shopping programs, programs are expanded, new locations open, shoppers move or quit, etc. Chances are that there are mystery shopping companies actively seeking mystery shoppers in your area.

Shops don't exist only in heavily populated areas. There may be more assignments available in a major city, but there are also more shoppers competing for those shops. In fact, you may find yourself in demand if you live in a sparsely populated area because it is often difficult to find shoppers in those areas. Do a good job, and you will be highly valued by mystery shopping companies and schedulers, who will give you as much work as they can.

The mystery shopping companies listed in this book aren't in my hometown. How can I find companies near me?

Most of the mystery shopping companies you will work for will not be located near you, even though they will hire you for shops in your town.

Many companies hire shoppers all over the country or even all over the world. For example, if a mystery shopping company is hired to shop all the locations of a national restaurant chain, they will need shoppers in every town that has one of those restaurants, including your town. But there are also local companies which shop only in your area. To find them, look in your Yellow Pages under "Shopping Services - Commercial" or similar headings.

Is the market saturated, or are there opportunities for new shoppers?

There is a lot of competition for mystery shopping jobs, but there are still opportunities for new shoppers. Mystery shopping companies must constantly recruit because businesses begin new mystery shopping programs, companies get new clients, current mystery shoppers quit or move to a different area, etc.

Additionally, most shops must be rotated among shoppers. For example, if a restaurant is shopped twice a month, and the client requires that a shopper may repeat the shop not more than once every three months, the mystery shopping company will need at least six shoppers (and probably more) just to handle that one location.

What do companies look for when they hire shoppers?

They want to know that you are reliable, observant and able to follow directions. You can demonstrate this by filling out the application accurately and completely. Shoppers need to be able to write comments and narratives, so they want to know that you can produce clear writing with correct grammar and spelling. Many will ask for a writing sample during the application process.

When selecting new shoppers, many companies give preference to shoppers who have earned MSPA Gold or Silver Certification. Find out more at http://www.mysteryshop.org/certification.php

Timeliness is important, so if a company contacts you respond promptly. If they contact you about an assignment, respond immediately.

Make it easy for mystery shopping companies to reach you by giving them more than one phone number (e.g., your home and office, a cell phone number).

Let them know what computer software (e.g., Microsoft Word, Excel, etc.) you can use, and if you have Internet access at home or at work. Give them your e-mail address. If you have a fax machine or scanner, that's a plus.

Other things that can help you get more shops include owning a digital camera, digital recorder or digital logger for telephone calls. A PDA or laptop computer may be useful.

Tell them when you are available. Can you only shop evenings and weekends or are you available anytime? Let them know how far you are willing to travel to do a shop. Most of the time they won't pay mileage, so let them know where (and how far) you are willing to go.

Give personal information. Are you married? Do you have kids? Grandkids? Pets? Do you wear glasses? What are your hobbies and interests? Do you own a car? Where do you like to shop? This is not the kind of information you would give on a job application, but it can help match you with assignments and get you more work.

How long will it take to get my first job?

If you apply to several companies, you may get your first shop within three to six weeks. Some shoppers have reported getting their first assignments the very same day they applied, but this isn't typical.

The more companies you apply to, the greater the number of shops you are eligible for and the sooner you will get an assignment. The more flexible and available you are, the more shops you can get.

Most of the time, you won't hear from a company unless they have a shop for you. So don't worry if you don't hear from some companies right away, or ever. It's probably not personal. They just don't have a need for shoppers in your area. You might consider e-mailing them or reapplying in six months or a year.

Is it ethical to work for more than one company?

Most companies understand that you will work for other companies. They know that they can't keep you busy all the time, and you want to work. Whatever you do, though, don't share information about one company with another, and don't share one company's report forms, completed evaluations, or other confidential information with another. Be professional and be discreet.

What will I do when I'm mystery shopping?

You'll be given specific guidelines for completing your mystery shop, and the company will provide instruction (usually in writing or over the phone). They will gladly answer your questions, so don't be afraid to ask. They want you to be comfortable doing the shop, and they want you to get it right.

While you are mystery shopping the business, you will be observing things about cleanliness, service, quality and other standards important to the business and its customers.

Questions on the evaluation might include things like: Were you greeted within 60 seconds? Were the floors clean? Did the person who took your order suggest additional items? Was the salesperson able to demonstrate product knowledge by answering your questions? Was your food fresh and served as you ordered it? Did the cashier count back your change and say thank you? Was the rest room clean and fully stocked with soap and tissue? When you leave the business, you will enter the answers on a report form or write a narrative report describing what you saw.

May I take my spouse, friend or child with me?

Sometimes, if it is a place they would normally go with you and if it is allowed by the mystery shopping company. Don't take anyone else along if they will distract you from properly completing your assignment, or if you have not been told that you may.

Remember you are a mystery shopper. If you have young children, don't tell them you're mystery shopping. You don't want them asking, loudly, in the middle of a shop, "Mommy, are we doing the mystery shop now?" Adults who accompany you must know that they are not to talk about mystery shopping or give away that you are the shopper.

Will the employees know that I'm the mystery shopper?

No. At first, you might feel like you have a neon sign that says MYSTERY SHOPPER blinking on your forehead, but they really won't know. If for some reason someone asks you if you are the mystery shopper, just say no or play dumb. "Mystery shopper? What's that?"

Will I be asked to do anything odd or to be "difficult"?

I've had to ask questions I thought were kind of silly, and I had to try to buy a pair of mismatched shoes (to see if the cashier caught it). But I've never been asked to make a scene, try to trick someone, be obnoxious, attempt to steal, or anything else that I wouldn't want to do. Each assignment will be explained to you. If you are at all uncomfortable with it, turn it down.

This sounds great! How do I get started?

Follow the Quick Start Plan on page 77 and start applying to companies. The more companies you apply to, the more shops you can get.

About the Author

Cathy Stucker has mystery shopped and educated mystery shoppers since 1995. She has helped thousands of people become professional shoppers.

When she's not shopping, Cathy Stucker is The Idea Lady™. She helps entrepreneurs, professionals, and authors attract customers and make themselves famous with inexpensive, creative and fun marketing.

Cathy has instructed courses for many colleges and universities, including the University of Houston, Collin County Community College, et al. She regularly presents seminars for continuing education programs and business organizations, and was selected by the Mystery Shopping Providers Association to develop and present the MSPA Gold Certification Workshops.

Cathy is a frequent media guest and has appeared on television and radio programs from coast to coast. She has been featured in *The Houston Chronicle*, *The Houston Business Journal*, *Black Enterprise*, *Woman's Day*, *Woman's World* and many others.

When she is not being written about, Cathy is writing. Her articles have been published in national magazines and other print and electronic publications.

For more information about Cathy Stucker, visit her on the web at http://www.IdeaLady.com/. To schedule a consultation or media interview, call Cathy at 281-265-7342. She may be reached via e-mail at cathy@idealady.com.

For updates and more information on
mystery shopping go to
http://www.IdeaLady.com/

Be sure to sign up for our
free e-mail course on
mystery shopping, and
get tips and hot news about
mystery shopping!